THE NOBEL BOOK OF ANSWERS

The Dalai Lama, Mikhail Gorbachev, Shimon Peres, and Other Nobel Prize Winners Answer Some of Life's Most Intriguing Questions for Young People

EDITED BY BETTINA STIEKEL

TRANSLATED BY PAUL DE ANGELIS AND ELISABETH KAESTNER

Atheneum Books for Young Readers

NEW YORK LONDON TORONTO SYDNEY SINGAPORE

Atheneum Books for Young Readers

An imprint of Simon & Schuster Children's Publishing Division

1230 Avenue of the Americas

New York, New York 10020

Translated from the German by Paul De Angelis and Elisabeth Kaestner

Originally published in Germany in 2001 as *Kinder fragen, Nobelpreisträger antworten*

by Wilhelm Heyne Verlag, Munich

First U.S. edition 2003

Book design by Ann Bobco

The text of this book is set in Garamond.

Printed in the United States of America

6 8 10 9 7

Library of Congress Cataloging-in-Publication Data

The Nobel book of answers: the Dalai Lama, Mikhail Gorbachev, Shimon Peres, and other Nobel Prize winners answer some of life's most intriguing questions for young people / edited by Bettina Stiekel.

p. cm.

Summary: A collection of essays written by various Nobel Prize winners about their fields of endeavor.

ISBN 978-1-4424-2193-6

1. Nobel Prizes—Juvenile literature. 2. Children's questions and answers.

[1. Nobel Prizes. 2. Nobel Prize winners.] I. Stiekel, Bettina.

AS911 .N9N567 2003

0011.4'4—dc21 2003008721

Contents

About the Nobel Prize

At his death on December 10, 1896, Alfred Bernhard Nobel, a Swedish scientist, established an international award to be given every year to the people who had "conferred the greatest benefit to mankind" for their achievements in physics, chemistry, medicine, literature, and peace. At that time, Sweden and Norway were united, and Nobel decided to divide the responsibilities for awarding the prizes. Organizations in Sweden were to award the honorees in science and literature. A Norwegian committee would award the annual prize for peace. The first awards were made in 1901, on the date of Alfred Nobel's death. (You can read more about the Nobel Prize in Mikhail Gorbachev's essay on page 1.)

In the years since the Nobel Prize was established, it has become recognized worldwide as one of the greatest honors a person can achieve in his or her lifetime.

Introduction
by Jimmy Carter

I was deeply honored to receive the 2002 Nobel Prize for Peace. The history of the prize has been a long and worthy one, and the award became especially important for me, and for all Americans, when it was given in 1964 to Martin Luther King Jr.

The first Nobel laureates whom I knew personally were Anwar Sadat and Menachem Begin. These two fine men, who were the leaders of their countries of Egypt and Israel, were honored for doing an extraordinary thing: They agreed to meet with me and talk about peace between their two countries. Up until then, Egypt and Israel had always been enemies, and my friends' decision was not popular with many people in their own countries. In fact, some people threatened to kill my friends for even thinking of meeting. Nonetheless, they met and we made an agreement at Camp David in 1978. Their courageous decisions led to the signing of an Egyptian–Israeli peace treaty that has never been broken by either side.

So, as you can see, while many Nobel laureates have carried out their work in safety, there are others who have acted with great personal courage. Two of my friends, Anwar Sadat, whom I mentioned earlier, and Yitzhak Rabin, the Israeli Prime Minister who won the Nobel Peace Prize in 1994, gave their lives for the cause of peace in the Middle East. Both men were assassinated by people with extreme views who disagreed with what Sadat and Rabin were trying to accomplish.

When I was president of the United States, I was one of the people who had the responsibility of keeping relationships stable during the height of the Cold War, when the world's two superpowers, the United States and the Soviet Union, opposed each other. Both sides understood that the stakes were enormous: a serious misunderstanding could lead to a nuclear holocaust. There had to be a constant and delicate balancing of both countries' great military strength with diplomacy.

In those days, the nuclear and military strength of the democratic United States and the totalitarian Soviet Union were almost equal. Ultimately democracy prevailed because of the people's commitments to freedom and human rights—not only by people in the United States, but also by people in countries allied with us, and by the people of the former Soviet empire as well.

The world has changed greatly since I left the White House. Now there is only one superpower, the United States, which has incredible military and economic strength. Thus our opinions are usually the ones that most influence worldwide decisions. With great power comes great responsibility. It would be a mistake to think that super strength guarantees super wisdom. So we as a nation must reach out to the international community to ensure that our own power and influence are balanced by the best common judgment.

In many ways, the world is now a more dangerous place than it was when I was president. We can communicate and travel to faraway places more easily than ever before—and yet we still have trouble understanding and respecting one another. All over the world there are civil wars in which the majority of the people killed are ordinary unarmed citizens, not soldiers. And the recent appalling acts of terrorism have reminded us that no nation—not even a superpower—is invincible.

So it is clear that peace is more important than ever. And while it may sometimes be imperfect, the best way to preserve global peace, and also to make change without violence, is through the United Nations.

During my years in the White House, I often thought of something a teacher once told me when I was a boy. Miss Julia Coleman would say, "We must adjust to changing times and still hold to unchanging principles." This same teacher also introduced me to Leo Tolstoy's novel *War and Peace*. She thought the book was a powerful reminder that the simple human gifts of goodness and truth can overcome great power. She also taught us that we as individuals have power. We don't have to be swept up by what happens around us. Every human being has the ability to influence even the greatest human events.

These ideas have been proven by the lives of many heroes who have been honored with the Nobel Prize: Albert John Lutuli, Norman Borlaug, Desmond Tutu, Elie Wiesel, Aung San Suu Kyi, Jody Williams, Albert Schweitzer, Mother Teresa, Martin Luther King Jr. All of these people and others have shown that even without government power—and often in opposition to it—individuals can fight for human rights. They can fight for peace, actively and effectively.

As you will see in these pages, Nobel Prize winners are interested in many things, from questions of medicine and theories of science to matters of the heart and mind. Nobel Prize winners are curious about the world around them, and their tireless search for answers to these questions have brought them success. Their discoveries, their work, always hold the highest purpose: to help people and to improve the quality of human existence.

I find hope in the growing belief that all people are entitled to certain things: peace, freedom, human rights, a clean environment, help for the suffering, and the rule of law. During the past decades, the international community, usually acting under the guidance of the United Nations, has tried to set global standards that can help nations achieve these essential goals for their people.

I also find hope in the unchanging principles in religion. As a Christian, I worship Jesus Christ, whose message was one of tolerance and love. I am convinced that despite their differences in specific beliefs, Christians, Muslims, Buddists, Hindus, Jews, and others—people of all the great religions—can embrace one another in a common effort to end human suffering and to promote peace.

At the beginning of this new millennium, I was asked to discuss the greatest challenge the world faces. I decided that the most serious problem is the growing distance between the richest and poorest people on Earth. The separation is growing every year—not just between countries, but also within them. As a result we are facing some of the world's biggest problems: illiteracy, starvation, environmental problems, unnecessary illness, violent conflict.

Sadly, in the industrialized world there is a terrible lack of understanding or even concern about what is happening to people who are enduring lives of despair and hopelessness in poorer lands. We have not yet made the commitment to share our wealth with others who desperately need it.

But one thing we all need—rich and poor alike—is peace. War may sometimes be a necessary evil. But no matter how necessary, it is always an evil, never a good. We will not learn to live with each other in peace by killing each other.

The bond of our common humanity is stronger than the divisiveness of our fears and prejudices. God gives us the ability to choose. We can choose to help end suffering. We can choose to work together for peace. We can make these changes—and we must.

JIMMY CARTER

I hope reading these essays inspires you to learn, think, and influence events according to your own unchanging principles.

Jimmy Carter was born in Plains, Georgia, in 1924. After having served as the thirty-ninth president of the United States, he and his wife, Rosalynn, founded the Atlanta-based Carter Center, a nonprofit organization that works to prevent and resolve conflicts, enhance freedom and democracy, and improve health around the world. In 2002 he received the Nobel Peace Prize for his decades of untiring effort to find peaceful solutions to international conflicts, to advance democracy and human rights, and to promote economic and social development.

How Do I Win the Nobel Prize?

by Mikhail Gorbachev

Dear Friend!

Do you know, actually, who invented the Nobel Prize? It was a Swede, Alfred Bernhard Nobel, himself a great scientist and outstanding inventor. He invented synthetic silk and welding with gas. His most famous invention was dynamite, and because he was not only a very smart man but also a very clever man, he opened his own manufacturing plant in which he produced dynamite. From there, he sold it to the whole world, and that is how he became very rich.

Shortly before his death, Alfred Nobel had an idea: He made a last will, and this will stated that nearly his entire immense fortune was to be used, after his death, to establish a foundation. This foundation would then have the task of awarding five large prizes each year to five outstanding men and women from the whole world—three of them for the most important discoveries or inventions in the areas of physics, chemistry, and biology or medicine. One prize was to be for literary works that, as he said, were "the most advanced toward 'the Ideal.'" A further prize was to go to the person who managed to create peace somewhere in the world—between two countries, for example, that had never gotten along and were at war. Much later, in 1968, a prize was started for economics, funded by the Federal Bank of Sweden on the occasion of its three-hundredth anniversary. Only the Peace Prize recipient is decided by a committee of the Norwegian Parliament; all of the other prizes are awarded by various Swedish organizations, including the Swedish Academy of Sciences.

Now, dear friend, you may think the whole thing is very strange and contradictory. A man who makes his fortune with dynamite, a deadly weapon, endows the world with prizes for things and works that are supposed to make the world wiser and happier—like, say, Albert Einstein's discoveries in physics, or Boris Pasternak's novel *Doctor Zhivago.* That the "King of Dynamite," as Alfred Nobel was called by his contemporaries, was the founder of a Nobel Peace Prize must seem totally contradictory to you. I myself don't consider it a paradox. Alfred Nobel was, after all, a man of great vision; shortly before his death, he was willing to learn from his own mistakes—something only very few are able to do. Late, but not too late in life, he understood that the fate of humankind was not supposed to be war, but peace. The same can be said of Andrei Sakharov, the ingenious Russian physicist and later a Peace Prize winner. At first Sakharov was one of the scientists who created nuclear weapons of unbelievable gruesomeness. Later on, however, he became one of the toughest and most uncompromising champions for nuclear disarmament, even risking his own health and freedom in the process.

So how do you become a Nobel laureate in the

first place? To answer this question, we may have to think about it somewhat differently. We have to think about who has become a Nobel laureate to date. Let's take some of the most famous whom you've heard about already or will hear about for sure—in physics class, for example. There, you will encounter the names of many Nobel Prize winners, names like Wilhelm Roentgen (who invented X rays—you probably know already what an X-ray machine is), Marie Curie, Niels Bohr, and Enrico Fermi. All of them, no doubt, are the founders of modern physics. Or let's look at another area of knowledge: biology or medicine. The names of people firmly intertwined with these disciplines are Ivan Pavlov, Robert Koch, and Alexander Fleming. And have you read any books yet by George Bernard Shaw, Thomas Mann, Ernest Hemingway, or Toni Morrison? If you haven't yet, you surely will—and not just because all of them received the Nobel Prize for literature for their great books, but because their books are truly great.

All right, those are just a few names. But I think

you already understand what I mean to say: that the men and women who have become Nobel laureates are only those who have enriched human knowledge through some extraordinary contribution, who have discovered as-yet-unknown laws of nature or unimaginable secrets of human life and of man's soul. In short, they are people who have opened truly new horizons for all of us.

Among the Nobel Prize winners so far—as you've already figured out by now—have been many politicians and scientists who brought people peace. Alfred Nobel, of course, thought through this part particularly well, for nothing is more difficult to understand than peace—and it is even more difficult for people to achieve. I know personally many recipients of the Nobel Peace Prize. All of them are wonderful, selfless people who spared no effort to end armed fighting, to restore peace and respect among people all over the world who seem to always be so senselessly embroiled with one another. To do this has never been simple or easy.

It is just as difficult as developing a complicated physics formula or solving an extremely challenging medical problem. Some Peace Prize winners have paid with their lives for their endurance and noble spirit—Martin Luther King Jr. or Yitzhak Rabin, for example. Or they struggled with difficulties—like Nelson Mandela, who sacrificed decades of his life in South Africa in the fight against apartheid. Nothing, not even prison and persecution, could dissuade him from his beliefs.

I do not want to make comparisons between myself and these men. But surely it was as much a surprise to them as it was to me when they learned that they had been awarded the Nobel Peace Prize. Why? Because everything they did was done for the sake of humanity, not because they were striving for recognition or even for some award. Understandably, one is all the more happy about such an honor. For it is happiness to see that one has really achieved something for people—and, above all, that the people have understood what one has oneself understood.

Do you want to know, my friend, what I understood? That war and violence were no longer supposed to be acceptable means in world politics, that no one should be threatened anymore with anybody else's weapons. From the moment that I was elected general secretary of the Communist Party of the Soviet Union and thereby head of the Soviet nation, the most important question for me was this: What could be done to put an end to the nuclear arms race? How could we avert, forever, the nuclear catastrophe that for so long already had hung over humanity like the sword of Damocles? I had to begin to transform my ideas into reality literally on the day I was elected, because the next morning a new round of Soviet-American negotiations on limiting weapons was supposed to start in Geneva. For years, people had sat together and not moved an inch. People were negotiating for negotiation's sake. So I declared that at last results were needed; and to show how seriously I meant business, I soon let the Americans know that in Europe we were willing to stop positioning the most dangerous midrange missiles—unilaterally and without any ifs, ands, or buts. Next ensued a long correspondence with then President Ronald Reagan, at first completely in secret and then a meeting with him in Geneva. At the end of these talks there were far fewer weapons in this world than before—and much more trust between two political systems that had been enemies up to then.

Whoever brings peace to others also receives it. This was another important lesson for me from those years. Only in the light of worldwide détente, a period of relaxed tensions, were we able to begin democratic changes in the Soviet Union, such as perestroika, a policy of economic reform, and glasnost, a policy allowing more freedoms. Yes, I believe to this day that a modern country must definitely try to bring the interests of its own people in step with those of the world community. Things were different in our country for a long time. Only after we no longer felt threatened, because we had stopped threatening others, could we warm to the idea that life was much richer and more complex than the best and most perfect governmental plans. The scheme into which communism had pushed people for seventy years was actually also a form of violence. After it had all ended, somebody in Stockholm picked up the receiver and called me.

Do you know now, dear friend, how one becomes a Nobel Prize winner? Do you perhaps want to become one yourself? If you really want to know, you will succeed. You must always remain curious, never accept an answer as final—and, above all, have faith in people, in their capacity for renewal, for solidarity, for poetry. And when one day you receive a Nobel Prize, I will take you to one of the conferences where Nobel laureates regularly meet. You and I will talk with the other laureates about how we can make people even a bit more thoughtful, science even a bit more revolutionary, literature even a bit more exciting.

Mikhail Gorbachev

And you will suddenly understand that your job as a Nobel Prize winner really only begins after you receive it.

Mikhail Gorbachev, born on March 2, 1931, received the Nobel Peace Prize in 1990 for his efforts to end the Cold War. He lives in Moscow and is chairman of the Foundation for Socioeconomic and Political Studies, which he founded.

Why Can't I Live on French Fries?

by Richard J. Roberts

When the Spanish conquered the Inca Empire in the sixteenth century, they found not only lots of gold among the South American Indians, but an edible plant with tuberous roots as well. Today, the potato has spread all over the world, and after rice, wheat, and corn, it counts as one of the most valuable foods of mankind. Artists have illustrated the potato, poets have praised it, monuments have been built for it, and there are even museums devoted to it. Many people were able to survive times of want because they at least had potatoes. Why, then, you ask, do your mom and dad object to your wanting to eat nothing but french fries every day, since, after all, they're made from potatoes? And they're on the menu of every fast-food restaurant.

The problem is everything that's been done to the potatoes before the crisp little golden yellow sticks land on your plate. Fast-food chains buy the potatoes from businesses that peel them in huge factories, cut them, briefly boil them in oil, then freeze them. Later they're thawed again in the fast-food shop, then fried in fat that's frequently much too old and usually far too heavily salted. Unfortunately, fries, unless they are fresh and expertly prepared, are not a very good source of nutrition. Pouring a lot of ketchup on top does not improve matters either.

But what is good nutrition? What does the body actually need to grow and do everything it needs to? What is a healthy meal made of? Well, you know from experience that if you devour a huge amount of ice cream or chocolate, your stomach will rebel—you'll get a stomachache or, in the worst case, you'll throw up. That means you ought not eat too much of one food. Another certain thing is that you should drink lots of water, since about two thirds of the human body consists of water. You can hardly survive a week without water. Finally, we know that each person must eat many different vitamins, minerals, proteins, fats, and carbohydrates. If any of these are lacking in the right combination for a long time, something can go seriously wrong in your body and you will get sick.

How much of each food type is exactly right? Obviously, no one answer applies to all people: A baby needs a different diet than an adult, a star athlete a different one than an old man. But even two boys of the same age and height do not necessarily need the same amounts of nutrients. As you may already know, the characteristics of each person are laid down in her or his genes, and these genes are different in everyone. Some people use foods very efficiently. We say they have a fast metabolism. Other people, by contrast, gain weight easily, although they eat no more than others. They digest more slowly.

Nobody knows exactly how genes cause one's

metabolism to be slow or fast, and experts in nutrition frequently have different opinions about it. The best idea is to listen to what your body tells you and to stick with what everyone knows: Don't eat too much. You don't need as much food as you think. Your stomach will "tell" you exactly how much—grumbling when it's hungry and feeling heavy when it's had too much food. What's more, be sure to eat a variety of foods. Some foods contain especially high amounts of a certain vitamin—carrots, for example. They contain beta-carotene, a substance the body transforms into vitamin A. Other delicacies may by comparison contain lots of a special protein. Fish, for instance, contains protein that is especially easy to digest. If fish or vegetables, and maybe fruit or salad, too, are part of your daily diet, so much the better.

So what's so bad about stuffing yourself with nothing but french fries all the time, anyway? Simple: Pretty soon you'll be missing important nutrients. Let's start with vitamins. The body does not need much of them, but in most cases, it cannot produce them. Potatoes contain mostly vitamin C and hardly any other vitamin. No vitamin K, for example, which is needed to form a scab when you're bleeding so that the bleeding stops. And no vitamin A, needed for the eyes to function properly. Not enough vitamin A, and you'll see even less well at night than everyone else. Over the long run a lack of vitamin A can even cause blindness. Many children in Africa suffer from it.

If you were to eat only french fries, your teeth would also slowly go bad and your bones would become brittle. That's because potatoes do not contain enough calcium, and your bones need calcium throughout your life, not just while you're growing. Besides, all those mountains of fries would overload you with sodium, because, as I mentioned earlier, they're often too salty and salt contains sodium. It's important that your body maintain a good sodium balance, because otherwise, it can't regulate its body temperature very well, but too much sodium causes high blood pressure in some people.

French fries also contain little protein. Proteins

are critical. They are the true bearers of life. The cells from which most living creatures are built consist mostly of proteins. Without proteins, for example, you would not have any muscles. Special proteins, called "enzymes," regulate the metabolism, and I'll tell you more about them in a minute. French fries at least supply the body with energy, because potatoes contain a lot of starches that belong to the carbohydrates group. For the human body, carbohydrates are like a heating-oil company.

You may now ask yourself: How, in fact, does the body take what it needs from food? How does metabolism work? Imagine you have a respectable house made of LEGO pieces, and you want to make something else with them. What do you do? You take the house apart, into single blocks. Then you can reassemble them again the way you want to. A similar thing happens with the body's metabolism. Step-by-step, nearly everything that people eat is made smaller inside the body. First the teeth do the job and later on mainly chemical reactions.

To get a better idea of what a chemical reaction is, read Klaus von Klitzing's essay in this book, which explains that all substances in nature consist ultimately of tiny atoms that very often combine into molecules. A molecule of the salt we use for cooking, for example, has one atom of sodium and one atom of chloride. That's why chemists call this salt "sodium chloride." Molecules, too, like to combine into even larger molecules. Proteins are good examples of such giant molecules. They're made of smaller molecules, the so-called amino acids. Different proteins get generated depending on which amino-acid molecules combine with which others to form chains and in which way.

So one atom can connect with another atom, and if both fit together, they can sometimes attach to a molecule—the same way you may fit a LEGO on top of the wall of your new house. You can also break up the connections between atoms or between molecules—the same way you can remove the LEGO from the wall of the house. This kind of construction, dismantling, and remodeling of molecules (the building blocks that constitute your nutrition) happens in the body all the time. Very special conditions have to be met, however, for this to happen so that metabolism functions. The body needs a lot of water for this, and a lot of energy. Energy comes mostly from fats and carbohydrates. But in order to work, metabolism needs, in addition, the enzymes already mentioned. Enzymes are what we chemists call "catalysts." They encourage chemical reactions to get going. Without their help, that would not happen, given our body temperature of about 98.6 degrees Fahrenheit.

Of course, when you eat fruits or vegetables, you don't think of what you're swallowing as molecules or building blocks. You eat spinach leaves, asparagus spears, or strawberries. All these are parts of plants that are themselves constructed, as are you, from many "LEGOs." All these building blocks are the raw materials out of which your body forms heart, lungs, stomach, bones, hair, and skin. The body, for example, gets amino acids from plant or animal proteins, and from them, it builds different and new proteins.

But back to the metabolic process during which your body gets the raw materials it needs. It starts in the mouth: When you put a fry into your mouth, the first thing you do is chew it with your teeth into large chunks and mix it up with saliva. The saliva contains enzymes that immediately start the job of breaking down the giant molecules. Then the mush slides into your stomach. There, strong acids and more enzymes are waiting to further disassemble the nutrients until they are small enough for the body to put them to its own uses.

But how do enzymes recognize the right nutrients out of all that food mush? you might now wonder. You know that enzymes are special proteins and that all proteins consist of amino acids. Enzymes, too, consist of amino acids that hook up with one another, forming long chains. The chains, in turn, fold up in such a way that they form small pockets. The chemical substances for which the enzymes are responsible fit exactly into these pockets. Let me explain this with an example of how starch is digested. In your body, the starch from french fries is transformed into sugar, which becomes a source of energy for the organism. If a sugar fits into the pocket of the relevant enzyme, it sits in it firmly, as in a vise, and the enzyme can go to work "unscrewing" single atoms. The enzymes split the bonds between the atoms of the sugar molecule, as we specialists say. In the process, the energy contained in the bonds is set free.

You know, of course, that our digestion does not happen only in the stomach. Food is processed all the way from the mouth, by way of the stomach, to the small intestine and the large intestine. At every station, as if along a lengthy conveyor belt, proteins and other helpers stand by to filter certain valuable substances from the mush of nutrients. Whatever cannot be used is eliminated again in the toilet. Whatever's useful, however, is transported to wherever the body needs it. Proteins, too, play a role in this transport. So-called epithelial cells are located along the walls of the digestive tract. They contain proteins that are equipped with pockets, just like the enzymes, and that can recognize amino acids or vitamins, for example. This time, the molecules are not "unscrewed" or disassembled in the pockets, but rather passed on—as in a relay race. This way, little by little, the substances get into your cells or directly into your blood. The circulation of the blood is especially important for transport across larger distances. After all, blood transports not only oxygen and nutrients, but also many other important substances, such as antibodies that fight against diseases.

In the past, people were mostly interested in "bad" bacteria, those that make us ill. Today, however, we know that some bacteria in our bodies are good for us. The best example is *Lactobacillus acidophilus,* which is contained in yogurt. You can even buy milk and yogurt drinks that dairies or the food industry have intentionally enriched with "good" bacteria. Thousands of different bacteria are swirling around in your intestine. They love sugars as well as roughage, also contained in potatoes. Each time you eat, new bacteria are added and others die or are eliminated. We don't understand all that well which of them we need to stay healthy. Ninety percent of these one-cell organisms inside the human body do not even have names. Nobody has studied them yet. Since one bacterium is ten times smaller than one cell in your body, you need very special equipment to look at it more closely. I have been trying for many years to find out more about these tiny mysterious little creatures. I'm especially interested in the enzymes that are produced by bacteria, which they use probably to protect themselves against their enemies, such as viruses. So if we study bacteria more closely, we also learn more about enzymes and thus automatically more about what role they play in human beings. Maybe with this kind of knowledge, we can invent new medications with which we can then fight contagious diseases triggered by bacteria.

As you can see, we chemists and doctors still know far too little about nutrition and its effects on health. This is why every person has to find out for him- or herself what's good for each. But one thing I can guarantee: You'll get into trouble if you always eat nothing but french fries. By the way, I myself would love to wolf down french fries every day. But I, too, have to restrain myself and should stick to the advice that I've given you here.

Richard J. Roberts was born on September 6, 1943. He received the Nobel Prize for medicine in 1993 with Phillip A. Sharp for the discovery of split genes. He is one of the directors of research at New England Biolabs in Beverly, Massachusetts.

Why Do We Have to Go to School?

by Kenzaburo Oe

Up to now I have thought about this question twice in my life. However troublesome, it's important to think thoroughly about important problems. And that's a good thing. Because even if a problem cannot be totally resolved, it becomes clear, looking back afterward, how important it was to have had enough time to think about it thoroughly. Fortunately, both times I thought over the question of why children have to go to school I came upon meaningful answers. They are, possibly, the best answers I have found to the innumerable questions posed in my life.

The first time I thought less about the reasons

why children have to go to school. Mostly, I had serious doubts about whether children should have to go to school at all. I was ten years old and it was autumn. In the summer of the same year, my homeland, Japan, had lost the war in the Pacific. Japan had fought against the Allies—against the United States, England, Holland, China, and other countries. And for the first time, nuclear bombs had been dropped on cities during this war.

Being defeated in the war led to big changes in the life of the Japanese. Until then, we children—and adults, too—had been taught that the supremely powerful Japanese Emperor, the Tenno, was a "god." After the war, however, it was announced that the Tenno was a human being.

I believed then that the changes were right. It made sense that a democracy created by all people with equal rights for all was better than a society that was ruled by a "god." I sensed this important change with all my soul, that it consisted of our no longer being forced to be soldiers, who killed people from other countries only because they had been declared to be our enemies—and who were themselves killed.

But one month after the end of the war I did not want to go to school anymore. You see, the teachers who had maintained until midsummer that the Tenno was a "god" and who had made us solemnly bow in front of his picture, teachers who had proclaimed further that the Americans were not people, but devils and monsters, now told us the opposite, without batting an eye. Not a word about their earlier way of thinking or method of instruction being wrong—or about whether they had even thought about it. They told us, as if it were totally natural, that the Tenno was a human being and that Americans were our friends.

On the day that soldiers of the occupation troops drove their jeeps into the little village in which I was born and raised, located in the middle of a totally wooded valley, the students stood on both sides of the road, waved their handmade starred-and-striped flags, and yelled "Hello!" I, however, sneaked away and went into the woods. From a high point, I looked down into the valley and observed how the jeeps drove along the road beside the riverbank, like miniatures. Even if I could not see the tiny little faces of the children, I could hear their voices shouting "Hello," and my tears flowed.

Although the next morning I headed for school, once I arrived, I made a beeline out the back door, ran into the woods, and stayed there until evening. I owned a huge picture book about plants. I searched the book for the exact names and characteristics of each tree in the woods and committed them to memory. Since my family was involved in managing the forest, it seemed a useful thing for my future life to know the names and identifying characteristics of the trees in the woods. There were many different kinds of trees in the forest. I was thrilled that each of the trees had its own name and special characteristics. Many of the Latin names of the trees that I memorized then, during that time in the woods, I still know today.

I did not want to go to school anymore. It would be enough to get me through life as a grown-up to thoroughly learn the names and characteristics of the trees while I was alone in the woods with my plant book. Besides, I knew that even if I did go to school, I would not find teachers or classmates there who were interested in the trees that fascinated me so much and with whom I could talk about them. Why did we have to go to school and learn things that had nothing to do with life as a grown-up?

One day in autumn, I went into the woods even though it was pouring rain. The rain got stronger and stronger, and streams sprang up all over the woods that had not been there before, and the path was buried under mounds of mud. It turned to evening, but I could not walk down into the valley. I became feverish and collapsed under a big magnolia tree. Two days later our village's fire department found me there and rescued me.

But once I was home, the fever did not go down. The doctor who came from the neighboring city said no method of treatment and no medicine could help me—I heard this news as if in a dream—and then he left. My mother was the only one who did not give up hope, and she nursed me. And one night I woke up from the condition I had been in—which had felt like a dream world wrapped in hot winds—and I realized that, though still feverish and weak, my head was clear again.

As is common in Japanese homes, I was lying on a futon that was spread out directly on the floor covered with tatami mats. My mother, who had probably not slept for several nights, was sitting at the head of the futon and looked down at me. Slowly and so softly that it seemed weird even to me, I tried to speak. "Mother, do I have to die?"

"I don't believe that you will die. I pray that you won't die."

"The doctor said, 'The child will probably die.' He said he couldn't do anything else for me. I heard it. I think I have to die."

My mother was silent for a while. Then she said,

"Should you die, I will give birth to you again. Don't be concerned about it."

"But if I die now, that child would be a different one than me."

"No, it would be the same," my mother said. "Once I give birth to the new you, I will tell the new you everything you have seen and heard up to now, all that you've read and all that you've done. And since the new you will also speak the language you are now speaking, the two children will be completely alike."

I had the feeling I did not really understand her. But it comforted me and I fell asleep. Starting the next day, I slowly began to recover. When winter came, I willingly went back to school.

While I sat in the classroom learning or was in the schoolyard playing baseball—a sport that became very popular after the war—I often became lost in thought. Was I not perhaps, here as I now was, the child whom my mother gave birth to after that sick and feverish child died? Could I not possibly be the new child to whom had been told everything that the other, deceased child had seen, heard, read, and done and who now experienced all this as a memory that had always existed within him? And was it not perhaps the language used by this dead child that I had now taken on and in which I was now thinking and talking?

Weren't the children in this classroom here and out in the schoolyard all children who were living in place of children who could not grow up but had died, these children having been told everything that those children had seen, heard, read, and done? The proof: We all spoke the same language. And didn't we all go to school to learn this language and make it our own? Still, to take on the language and the experiences of these deceased children, we didn't have to learn just Japanese, but also science and math and even sports! If I went into the woods alone to compare the trees there with those in my plant book, I couldn't step into the place of the dead child and become a new child who was identical to the earlier one. That's why we all go to school, learn, and play together.

Maybe this story that I've told you strikes you as a bit strange. Though this experience came back to me after a long time, today as an adult, even I do not totally understand anymore what I understood perfectly well when I was finally healthy and went to school again with a quiet pleasure at the beginning of that winter. Yet I tell you this memory, which I have never before written about, in the hope that you who are now children—new children—are perhaps able to really understand it.

Something else I remember is an experience I had as an adult. My oldest child, a boy named Hikari, was born with a malformed head. He had a huge bump at the back of his head so that it looked as if he had two heads, a big one and a small one. The doctors removed this bump, careful to damage his brain as little as possible in the process, and closed the wound.

Hikari grew quickly, but he still could not talk when he was four or five years old. He was especially sensitive to the pitch and the tone of sounds. What he learned first was not human speech, but the different songs of the birds. Soon when he heard the sound of a specific bird, he could also say the name of that bird, which he knew from a recording of bird songs. That's how Hikari began to talk.

Hikari started school when he was seven, a year later than normal children, in a "special" class. In the class were children with various disabilities. Among them were children who screamed the whole time. Others could not sit still and had to run around the whole time, bumping into tables and kicking over chairs. Whenever I looked in through the window, Hikari was cupping his ears with both hands and was holding his whole body rigid.

So once again, as an adult, I asked myself the same question I had asked myself as a child: Why does Hikari have to go to school? He knows the songs of the birds very well and enjoys learning their names from his parents. Wouldn't it be better if we went back to our village and lived in a house we built on the upper meadow in the woods? I would look up the names and identifying signs of trees in the plant book, and Hikari would listen to bird songs and recite their names. My wife would make drawings of us both and cook for us. Why was this impossible?

But it was Hikari himself who solved this difficult problem for me, the adult. Sometime after Hikari entered the special class, he found a friend who, just like him, hated loud sounds and noises. From then on, the two of them always sat together in a corner of the classroom and held hands while they endured the noise in the classroom. Besides, Hikari's friend was physically weaker than he was, and Hikari helped him when he had to go to the bathroom. This experience of being useful to his friend was a newfound happiness for Hikari, who at home was dependent on his parents for every little thing. Soon you could see the two sitting on their chairs next to each other at something of a distance from the other children, listening to music broadcasts on the radio.

After one year Hikari realized that the language he knew best was no longer the songs of birds, but the music composed by people. He even brought home slips of paper on which his friend had written the names of pieces they liked from the radio program, and he searched for these records. The teachers realized that words like "Bach" and "Mozart" occurred in the conversation between these two boys, who otherwise were almost always silent.

Hikari went through "special" classes and special education together with his friend. In Japan school ends in the twelfth grade for students with mental handicaps. At the ceremonies on graduation day we parents heard the teachers tell Hikari and his fellow students that, starting tomorrow, there would be no more school.

During the party that followed, Hikari, who was given to understand several times that there would be no more school starting tomorrow, declared: "This is strange." To which his friend answered, from the depth of his heart: "Yes, this is strange." There was a smile on both of their faces that expressed surprise but at the same time radiated calm.

Taking this little dialogue as a starting point, I wrote a poem for Hikari, and he, who had received music instruction initially from his mother and who meanwhile was composing himself, turned it into a piece and gave it to his friend as a gift. The composition with variations that developed from this, titled "Graduation," has by now been performed at several concerts and found many listeners.

Today, music is for Hikari the most important language for discovering the depth and richness of his inner being, for communicating with others, and for defining himself in relation to society. The seed was planted in his family, but only in school could this seed unfold. Not only Japanese, but also science and math and even sports and music are languages that are necessary in order to really understand oneself and be able to make connections with other people. The same is true for foreign languages.

I believe that, to learn all this, children have to go to school.

Kenzaburo Oe, born on January 31, 1935, received the Nobel Prize for literature in 1994 for his work as a whole. He lives in Tokyo and teaches all over the world as a visiting professor. His first novel since receiving the Nobel Prize, *Somersault*, was published in English in the spring of 2003.

Why Are Some People Rich and Others Poor?

by Daniel L. McFadden

Some people have more money than others—I'm sure you've often noticed that yourself. Some of your classmates are brought to school in huge cars, while others come by bus. Some wear designer duds; others, old clothing worn thin. I'm sure some have expensive gadgets that you'd also love to have, but your parents don't want to buy them for you, maybe because they can't afford them.

When I was young, it was clear to me that I owned far fewer things than many other children. My family was very poor—we did not even have electricity on our farm in northern California. My parents, however, were not ashamed to be poor. On the contrary: They did not like rich people. Too much money, they were convinced, would spoil one's character. They taught me that there were more important things in life than a brand-new bicycle. So I grew up without the idea that I had to become rich. Meanwhile, it turned out that I can live pretty comfortably on account of my profession—I'm a professor of economics at a university. Still, all the years I've done research on how prosperity is acquired and distributed in our society have only made me more convinced of what my parents taught me back then.

I say this at the very beginning of this essay because I believe that it is absolutely necessary for you to understand this when you think about why some people are rich and some are poor. After all, many people believe that money can solve all problems. They admire billionaires like Bill Gates and secretly wish they could have a bank account as fat as his. Maybe they even go so far as to consider poor people less worthy. But that is wrong. You should judge people not by their pocketbooks, but by their characters and personalities only. Artists and social workers, for example, knowingly choose a career in which they won't earn very much, simply because they like their work. I've often noticed that people like this are happier than those who are always only running after money. Whether or not it is at all desirable to become rich is a decision you'll have to make as you grow older.

But why are there rich people and poor people? Of course we ask that question anyway, even if we don't want to become rich. Maybe you once saw a homeless person and wondered: Why does this person have to live on the street? Where does he sleep? Where does he get something to eat? Or maybe you saw a report on TV about Africa; many people over there own practically nothing. Why are they so badly off? How did this happen?

Whether people are rich or poor is first and foremost a matter of luck. If you are lucky enough to grow up in a well-to-do country like the United States or the United Kingdom, you are already pretty well off—in any event, better off than most children in Africa. Maybe you're lucky enough also to have parents who own a pretty house with a yard and who go to the beach with you over vacation. Maybe one day you'll even inherit the assets your parents have accumulated—that would mean you get a lot of money without having done anything for it yourself. You see: It's all a matter of pure luck.

In Africa many people are so poor that they do not even have enough to eat. In most cases, these people could not have helped it, either. Often, poverty is created by war: The usual economic processes are destroyed, and people cannot go about their jobs anymore because, for instance, they are refugees. However, it can be very, very difficult to make money in Africa even in times of peace; in many countries, for example, it rains so rarely that hardly anything grows in the fields. Children whose parents are poor farmers have hardly any other opportunity but to become poor farmers themselves. Just as you can inherit riches, so can you inherit poverty.

Perhaps you are lucky enough also to have been born with a special talent. If you are, say, an excellent soccer player, you could possibly earn a great deal of money. People with extraordinary abilities are usually richer than those without. If you live in Africa, however, you might never have the opportunity to develop such a talent. You might be an awesome soccer player or a math genius—and you would still stay poor because nobody would notice your talent.

So there's another instance of luck: the opportunity to receive a good education and to have the chance to develop your talents. Of course, sometimes you'd rather do something else than go to school. And when your parents say then that school is really important, you don't believe them. But they are right. It's a great privilege to go to school in America or England. The education you receive is considerably better than in many other countries. By the way, people who have a good education usually make more money and become richer. At some point in your life what happens to you is not just a matter of luck anymore. At that time, you yourself can influence your standard of living by choosing a job that brings in more or less income.

Basically, there are three ways to acquire income. The first and most important source is by selling your capacity to work to somebody else. If you become an automobile mechanic, a doctor, or a professor, you are going to be paid for what you do. This is the main source of income for most people. The sum of money they get paid for their work decides whether they become more or less wealthy.

The second source of income comes from owning something that has productive value. For example, if you rent a truck to a contractor who's building a house, you receive rent—that is to say, income—because you own the truck.

The third major source of income and prosperity arises from people's entrepreneurial talents: They invent new things and establish new companies to sell their products. Look at Bill Gates. He's rich because his company offered a new product that proved extremely successful. Innovation can be one of the most exciting opportunities for a young person. And you don't need to be a computer freak either. Come up with an idea as utterly normal as how to improve the placement of goods onto supermarket shelves, and as long as you convince others to use your method, you may even get rich.

I'm well aware that possibilities like these to acquire an income work well for some and not at all for others. Even in a rich country like the United States, you will always have people who are relatively poor. Sometimes it's because of illness. Sometimes, though, it's due to lack of willpower or self-control. By using drugs, some people rob themselves of the chance to lead a normal life and have a good income. But there are also large numbers of people who are unemployed—they are well trained and would love to work, but they do not find employment. Why don't you ask your parents whether they know anybody who's unemployed? More people have had to get through that kind of thing than you might imagine.

Maybe you think all of this is not fair. I can only agree with you. Unfortunately, there's hardly anything to be done about it—the world's not fair, and that's all there is to it. I know it's hard to accept this fact. But there's no way to kid ourselves about this point: Over several thousand years, people have not come up with an economic system that distributes resources evenly enough so that no one is poor. The economic system in Europe, the United States, and many other countries is called a "market economy." That means that companies can manufacture the things they want to produce and that people are free to buy what they want to buy. The economy is regulated not by the government, but by the market itself. The system works because people are eager to assert their own interests. If word gets around that a particular product is needed, somebody will likely manufacture it. For instance; if everybody suddenly wants to buy soccer balls and the stores run into a shortage of them, it's very likely that somebody will soon produce more soccer balls to meet the increased demand. They will do it because they can make good money from the soccer balls.

A market economy has many advantages. To a large extent, you yourself have control over what will happen to you. If you don't like a product, you don't have to buy it. A market economy also has disadvantages, however. The biggest one is that it is by no means fair to everybody. A market economy does not protect people against blows of fate. Many jobholders in a particular sector of the economy may be very committed and industrious. But if this sector collapses for some reason having to do with the total economic system, they lose their jobs. It is not fair, but it happens again and again. That is the downside of a market economy.

Perhaps you're now thinking: Why don't all the Nobel Prize winners in the world get together and invent a system that is really just? A system where nobody has to be poor? Well, that's exactly what "communism" is about. Maybe you've already heard that term. The idea behind it is that everyone decides jointly how goods will be distributed and everybody does it for the good of the group. Sounds good, doesn't it? Communism was practiced in Russia for over seventy years, but the communist economy collapsed in 1990. The system simply did not work. The collapse of communism proved that this concept is subject to two big problems. First, the individual in communism is not given as much of a direct and powerful incentive to work as in a market economy. Even if you care about others, it's difficult to get up in the morning and work really hard if it brings you no direct benefit. However sad, I believe this is part of human nature.

The other problem with communism comes from how goods are distributed. In theory, it sounds good to say that everyone will decide jointly about these issues. But in practice, some kind of bureaucracy is needed to make the decisions. History has shown that at some point the public gets fed up with being passed over by this bureaucracy and it rebels against it. Besides, the bureaucracy in this kind of system does not have access to the information needed to make such decisions, and it does not experience the same kind of incentive to care for individuals that the individuals themselves do. Whenever I look after myself, I have a real incentive to see to it that I get what I want. If I'd rather eat whole wheat than white bread, I have an incentive to go out and look for whole wheat bread. If a central bureaucracy controls the distribution of goods, however, the bureaucracy won't get the message that it should give me whole wheat rather than white bread.

So it looks pretty much as if all we have left is the market economy. Despite all its disadvantages, it's probably the best economic system people have come up with so far. You should realize, though, that slicing up the wealth is no picnic. It's a difficult affair, something of a fight. People have different interests, they wrestle with one another and that means that there are winners and losers—rich and poor.

Governments in many western European countries, for example, supplement the market economy by putting out a safety net for people who have had a lot of bad luck. The government can see to it that poor people are not too poor. I believe that civilized countries look after people who are stuck in social difficulties fairly well.

So, the government uses tax revenues—the money it gets when people pay their taxes—to make sure that the poor don't wind up in too lousy a spot. Should you try to use the politics of taxation to make sure that all people wind up at the same level, however, you would wipe away all the incentives that stimulated the market economy in the first place. People who work hard, have a good education, and quickly develop their abilities need incentives to achieve a higher income. If people had a guaranteed income whether or not they worked, many would not work as hard or would not work at all.

I hope you are not too disappointed now that you've reached the end of this essay. I had meant to explain why some people are rich and some are poor. In the end, it all boils down to one sentence: The world is not fair. After all, we people are selfish creatures; we think first of ourselves and only later—maybe—about others. This especially hits me whenever I apply my moral standards to my own standard of living. It makes me sad to see people drive huge cars and build showy homes when there are so many people who are really, really poor. Still, I have to admit that I myself have a pretty nice home, too, and a pretty big car. I think to myself over and over again that I wouldn't mind if I were not well off. But I'm not totally sure about it.

Daniel L. McFadden was born on July 29, 1937. He received the Nobel Prize for economics in 2000 for his theory of "discrete choice"—a theory that, among other things, can predict how a majority of the population would behave if given a limited number of options. He teaches at the University of California at Berkeley.

Why Do We Have Scientists?

by John C. Polanyi

I don't really know anymore exactly why, as a child, I was so interested in science. Maybe because I always loved to ask questions. Every young child asks "Why?" a hundred times a day. Curiosity is as natural to humans as it is to animals. Babies are curious, dogs and cats are curious. All of us find it exciting to look into closed boxes or under rocks to find out what's hidden. A door creaks, and the guessing game in your mind starts instantly: *Who's coming? Is it my mother? My brother?* Every human being longs for explanations. We scientists don't call them "explanations," but instead call them "theories."

But why are we that way? Why do we always want to have a reason? Why do we need a theory for everything? Three thousand years ago, Socrates, a Greek who serves as an example for every scientist, answered the question of why he became a philosopher by saying that unless he explored himself and everyone else, his life would have no meaning.

We all start out experiencing the reality around us as a mixture of different impressions, such as sunlight, warmth, the rustling of the wind in the trees. As long as we have been on Earth, we humans have thought up one story or another that brings order to these images and impressions that otherwise seem unrelated. The type of story we scientists tell is only one kind of many; other people tell stories in the form of fairy tales, plays, novels, or poems. Our science stories are often about how one state of affairs connects to an entirely different one in a wholly surprising way. An example: Without the warming rays of the sun, there would be no cooling winds. And without sun and wind, green leaves and trees would have no energy to live.

Like all good stories, the one about the sun, the wind, and the trees has a clear form: that of a circle. You know, of course, that human beings and animals—you and I included—breathe in the oxygen that plants give off. In turn, we all exhale carbon dioxide, which is what plants need. They nourish us and we nourish the plants. Nature had a good idea when it invented this cycle, and it will go on like that for all of eternity—provided we human beings don't meddle with it too much. Just imagine if we cut down all the forests on this Earth. Not only would that be the end of all trees, but the oxygen essential for life would be gone. So if we disturb the balance, both suffer: the plants and us as well.

So is that what scientists do? Tell stories all day long and search for a connection among everything we experience day in and day out? In a way, yes; but some other things are tied in with our work that are just as important and are lots of fun for me.

Why exactly is my work so much fun? Because it's

connected to magical forces that spur us researchers to achieve fantastic things over and over again. When I say that, I don't mean to suggest that we are actually magicians, since we're limited by, among other things, what's possible. (That reminds me of a letter from a group of Swedish pupils that I received shortly after I was awarded the Nobel Prize for chemistry: "Dear Professor, Congratulations on your prize. Our chemistry class has a request: Could you stop by and blast our school into the air?" To these students, I was a sorcerer who could chase away their boredom by blowing up their school.) No, I mean something else when I talk about the magic of science: the magic of numbers. Science is concerned with things you can somehow count or calculate. If a scientist were to give a description of you, for example, he would not say that you are pretty or that you are honest, but that you are about four feet seven inches tall and that you weigh ninety-nine pounds.

Now you have an idea why the kids in Sweden wanted me to blow up their school so badly: The scientist's way of describing people is awfully boring. It has the advantage, however, of making certain stories possible that otherwise could never be told. Using the method we call "arithmetic," for example, we can say how tall and how heavy your classmates are on the average, even though we can't say anything about their looks. You see, on the one hand, numbers limit us—I couldn't say anything about why your laughter is so contagious, for instance, no matter how many numbers I use. On the other hand, numbers make our statements more precise. We scientists don't say, "My father has huge feet." Instead, we say, "My father's shoe size is 12E."

Or take Albert Einstein. If Einstein had said only that something we call "mass" (how heavy something is) relates to something we call "energy" (a name for movement), it would all have sounded good, but nobody could really have done much of anything with it. But since Einstein calculated that a very specific small mass could produce a very specific, incredibly huge amount of energy, he said something we could understand. Perhaps you already heard somewhere of his famous theory of relativity? That's exactly what I'm talking about. Einstein's theory was so utterly correct that in a very short time many, many scientists could use his calculations and had ideas about how to prove his theory.

And that changed the world. First, the theory of relativity gave us new ways to blow things up: Scientists developed the "atomic bomb," which is called that because it converts the mass of an atom into energy for use as a weapon. (Science can have terrible consequences—I'll come back to that later on.) The same clever idea showed us the way to obtain a huge amount of electricity out of a tiny bit of uranium. That meant a great improvement for everyday life. And yet it also meant danger, because even nuclear power plants can explode, as we know from the accident at the nuclear plant at Chernobyl in Ukraine in 1986. Sooner or later, we'll succeed in extricating much larger quantities of energy from one or two drops of water, with much less danger.

Scientists are now at work on developing a machine that can do this—a fusion reactor—and it's only a question of time before they succeed.

When we say that science can sometimes be dangerous, we also have to think about what we can do against the danger. How can we make sure that nothing worse happens because of our work? I've already said that some people see us scientists as sorcerers. And it's not hard to imagine how, like the sorcerer in fairy tales, we are unable to stop our own magic. Usually, science tells us something about nature, like why the moon is sometimes a quarter moon, sometimes a half moon, and sometimes a full moon. Or why Australians, who live on the opposite side of the Earth, don't fall off. Why nobody grows to be thirty feet tall. The answers to such questions are often so clever that they lead us to new and more intelligent questions and then to even more intelligent answers.

When we talk about controlling science, it isn't a matter of stopping scientific inquiry, but of controlling what we do with our new knowledge. Do we use Einstein's discovery that we can turn mass into energy to build atomic bombs in order to kill people? Or do we use this knowledge to make people's lives less burdensome? This is not a decision made by scientists alone, but by the whole of society, by the politicians, by people who vote, by everyone. Well, maybe not children, since they still have to learn how the world functions before they're given the chance to decide what should be different about it.

Scientists can help explain the world to children and all others and help improve it. For hundreds of years, discovering the truth has been more important to them than the question of who made the discovery. This does not mean that scientists do not quarrel with one another—they fight like crazy! Everybody wants to be the next to win the Nobel Prize. So it's all the more amazing that none of us keeps our knowledge to ourselves: Everyone shares with and mutually supports one another no matter what country they come from and what God they believe in. The international community of scientists is something wonderful, and it is a great honor for me to be part of it.

I get paid for researching things, even if it sometimes looks as if I'm playing. My newest toy, for example, is a machine for tickling molecules. With a laser beam, I aim at the molecules—a tightly connected group of atoms—and can watch how they react: One atom after the other separates from the pile and forms new molecules. Unfortunately, this toy has cost me a lot of aggravation because on most days it doesn't work at all. Pretty annoying, since I'm expected to be discovering something new all the time if I want to continue to be a science researcher—and I want that more than anything.

You can imagine how excited I was when this stupid machine finally did what it was supposed to do and my students and I could get a look at something no person had ever seen before. For a brief moment we had a glimpse of what tremendous joy, and what relief, an explorer like Christopher Columbus must have felt when, after several months' journey at sea, he suddenly sighted land. At the moment that he had given up all hope, he found America. After taking our molecules apart and putting them back together again, we felt the same way.

Maybe now you'll ask: What's the best way to become a science researcher? The most important thing is, you really have to want it. The most different kinds of people with the most different kinds of talents become scientists, but they all have one thing in common: They do their research with great passion and with all the energy they possess.

Just in case you're worried that over the next years scientists in their enthusiasm will discover everything there is to be discovered and that nothing will be left for you, let me reassure you: What we know today is just a tiny part of what we still have to find out. Inside the nucleus of the cells of humans, animals, and plants, inside the atoms and at the edge of the universe, there are many new worlds waiting to be discovered by someone.

Maybe that someone is you.

John C. Polanyi, born January 23, 1929, received the Nobel Prize for chemistry in 1986, along with Dudley R. Herschbach and Yuan T. Lee, for research on the dynamics of chemical reactions. He teaches at the University of Toronto.

What Is Love?

by H.H. Dalai Lama

What is life all about? Buddha, a monk who lived more than two thousand years ago, had a very simple answer: We all want to be happy. Yet how do you become a happy person? Many people believe that they have achieved it once they are rich or famous or have as much power as possible. However, they often realize later on that life, even with lots of money and luxury, is still just as meaningless and empty as before. Buddha's recipe for happiness is stunningly simple: Try to become a good person. Since that's easier said than done, he offered a few tricks, like a good trainer.

It all starts in your own head. You have to change your attitude, your way of thinking: to do right and avoid wrong. We were not born into the world to harm others. Only by meeting every person with a warm heart and in friendship does our life have meaning. That is the foundation of my philosophy. The key to everything is love. But what is it, this thing we call "love"? Every day we hear the word "love" a thousand times. In the morning a voice on the radio chirps, "I love you." At midday you might say the word, with your heart racing, to a boy or girl you have a crush on. At night your mother whispers it into your ear and gives you a good-night kiss. Surely you've also heard your father say that he loves his car or his video collection.

Still: Is everybody here talking about the same kind of love? I don't think so. Many people confuse love with pleasure or a momentary feeling of attraction to a person (or to a thing). This kind of love is unsteady and moody, like the weather. We love somebody because he has such beautiful eyes, because of the wise things she says, or for a thousand other reasons we have imagined. Later, when the sun stops shining, we realize that this kind of love was pure wishful thinking. It's similar with toys or clothes. An example: You go into a store, you suddenly see something you like, and you say, "I want it." At this moment, an affection begins and turns this ordinary object into something special. You buy the object and you realize, now that you own it, that it looks even more beautiful. It's still the same thing you can find many times over in the store, but now that it's in your pocket, you start to love it, because it is only yours. In this case, love is nothing but possessive thinking.

Most people dream of romantic love as wonderful as in a Hollywood movie. Two people meet, all sorts of sparks fly, already they're blinded by love. Love crazy. Unfortunately, experience shows that relationships or marriages that emerge from this kind of love rarely last. A passionate relationship is indeed like a house built on ice. As soon as the ice melts, the building collapses. This kind of love can turn easily into tediousness and boredom. At worst, it can turn into hatred. This, unfortunately, happens all too easily between people who once loved each other. And so this, too, is not real, true love.

A couple in love once asked me, "Can we expect that our partner loves us back?" My answer: "No." That would be like a barter: If you love me, I love you too. That's the wrong attitude. In my opinion, love is something else altogether. True love is free of jealousy, free of conditions, and it knows no prejudice. This kind of affection is a little like what Jesus called "love for thy neighbor."

Something like a seed of love lies dormant in every person. This seed lives in our hearts, and we can make it grow and later on see to it that it blooms like a flower. We monks do this by practicing positive acts. Tolerance and respect for the environment are part of this, and, of course, you're not supposed to commit bad deeds like killing, stealing, or lying. You don't have to be a saint to cultivate warm and friendly relations with other people. The love I refer to applies to all creatures on our planet. That's why I ask you: Is there any difference between love for a mother and love for an ant? No!

Even if it sounds unbelievable to you, it is possible to love your enemies. It is even very important to learn to love your enemies. Normally, you consider somebody who annoys you and causes you trouble your opponent. That is wrong. No matter, he or she is still a human being. Given that we love humankind, how can we exclude enemies? We have to extend our hand to them as well as to our friends.

I do admit that it is difficult to love your enemies. I can give you an example, however: When I was fifteen years old, in 1951, the Chinese army marched into Lhasa, the capital of Tibet. I tried to find a peaceful solution to the conflict because I was the spiritual and political leader of my people. But I tried in vain, unfortunately. In 1959 Mao Tse-tung's Communist troops killed thousands of my countrymen and occupied the whole nation. I myself fled across the Himalayan mountains into neighboring India, where I have lived in exile ever since. The Tibetan people, therefore, have every reason to hate the Chinese for the unimaginable suffering they caused our people. But whenever such feelings arise in us, we turn inward. We try to develop compassion for the Chinese, too. An enemy remains a person, no matter what he or she has done. As an individual, as a human being, he continues to deserve our respect and our love. We do, however, condemn his ill-intended acts. If necessary, we also have to protect ourselves from them.

Surely you now want to know, How do we learn how to love? There is no recipe and no formula. For me, it's a bit like the art of cooking. Every dish needs to be prepared in a different way and requires a special touch. For one dish, you may have to precook the vegetables, then fry them, and add the spices at the end. For another dish, you might start with a solid dash of salt. When you want to make a success of a delicious meal, you always have to consider different aspects. It's no different when dealing with people.

So for me, too, it's therefore not enough to say: "Hello. From now on, be more loving and compassionate with one another." To me, the most effective method is to put yourself into the other person's place, to imagine what he thinks and how he feels. How he suffers.

That's why we monks have daily practices to develop and strengthen our capacity to feel as others do. We imagine a situation in which a feeling creature suffers. It might be a sheep about to be slaughtered. We try to imagine the suffering the sheep has to endure. The anxiety of being killed, the pain, the blood.

Or imagine a situation in which a loved one suffers. Ask yourself then how you yourself would react. In this way, you can learn how to better understand the feelings and experiences of other people and to develop empathy and concern for them.

The ability to put oneself into the other's place and to think about how we would behave in that place is very useful if we want to learn how to love someone. But this technique also requires a great deal of courage. It takes courage to imagine how it would feel to be in the other's skin. This often helps to take the bite out of a quarrel, since it's a way to better understand unfamiliar feelings and to learn to respect them.

It's good when love lives in our hearts. It's a good thing to truly wish that others be free of suffering and that there be no more aggression and hatred. The word for "empathy" in the Tibetan language is *Tse-wa*. You can also translate *Tse-wa* as "respect" or "responsibility." A further meaning for this word in our language is "wishing oneself good things." The simplest way to do this is to first wish yourself to be good and free from worries. Then allow the feeling to grow in you; when it has grown big enough, you can let it become larger and larger and, in the end, infect other people with it.

You see, this form of love is independent of whether or not you like this person or that. Every creature has an inborn wish to be happy. Each has the same right as you or I do for this wish to be fulfilled. So whenever I get together with other people, I approach them with this feeling. I know we have many things in common that connect us together: We all have a body, a soul, and feelings. We are all born to a mother. We all have to leave this world one day. Every one of us wishes ourselves happiness, not misfortune, in life—no matter our skin color, religion, or size of our shoes.

Looking at people from this point of view allows me to feel that the person I am meeting is just like I am myself.

His Holiness the Fourteenth Dalai Lama (meaning "Ocean of Wisdom") was born on July 6, 1935. He received the Nobel Peace Prize in 1989 for his efforts on behalf of human rights in Tibet. He is the spiritual and secular leader of the Tibetan people and is considered to be the reincarnation of the Buddha of Compassion. He has lived in exile in India since 1959.

Text by: Yu-hui Chen and Michael Cornelius, from an interview with the Dalai Lama on July 28, 2000, in Dharamsala, India.

Why Do We Feel Pain?

by Günter Blobel

When I was a little boy, my mother read to me from a big book of fairy tales. There were elephants and tigers, enchanted princes and magic carpets. But most of all, I loved the fakirs of India. The picture in my book of fairy tales showed one such Indian fakir in his silken pants, a magnificent turban on his head. He was sitting on a board with thousands of sharp nails sticking out of it, his dark almond-shaped eyes laughing out of his light brown face. "Fakirs know no pain," my friend explained, and I believed him.

Today, I know that this is not the case. Just like you and me, fakirs feel it when something hurts them, even though they look different from white

Europeans or dark Africans. They can only learn to suppress their pain. Don't let external appearances deceive you: All people are pretty much the same no matter how different they may look. The same blueprint lies behind black or blond hair, behind gray eyes or high cheekbones. Nature developed this blueprint for all living creatures many millions of years ago. At the time people did not even exist yet. This blueprint is the reason why everyone can experience pain—not only people, but animals, too.

Why are we human beings all so similar to one another and equally sensitive to pain? Picture it this way: The human body consists of many, many building blocks, called "cells." Each cell, in turn, contains tiny little machines that accomplish various tasks: They process nutrients; they produce energy, giving strength to our muscles; they send messages back and forth; and they cleanse the cells of substances that are not needed anymore. By the way, these machines exist not only in humans, but also in animals, plants, and bacteria.

You may be only ten or eleven years old, but in reality—imagine!—you are already three and one half billion years old. Way back then is when the first cell began to live. It divided and divided again, and the new cells that were created that way got together and worked as a team. And that's how the first living creatures evolved. Sponges, for example, are multicellular organisms that swim in the ocean. More and more complicated creatures evolved from them—plants, animals, and finally, human beings.

You yourself started as two tiny cells: the egg cell of your mother and the sperm cell of your father. Both carried half a blueprint, and they merged during conception. The result was your "ancestral cell." This ancestral cell then began to divide. The more often it divided, the more you grew—at first still inside your mother's womb, then outside after birth. By then, you already consisted of billions of cells, and you had not even stopped growing. You need that many cells not only to reach a height of, say, six feet, but also because your body is made up of many different parts that can accomplish their tasks only with these cells' help. You have organs, like your heart, for example, which is responsible for pumping the blood through your body. You have a brain, which is supposed to solve complicated math problems. And you have skin, hair, nails, eyes, and much more. All these body parts consist of cells.

The miracle of "evolution"—the name for the continuous unfolding of life since its beginning billions of years ago—lies in the organization of these cells in such ways that enable them to accomplish their varied tasks. We scientists do not yet completely understand how this happens exactly, but we are discovering more and more of the details. We know, for example, that every cell has a nucleus that contains the blueprint. We inherited it from our parents, just as they inherited it from their parents, grandparents, and so on. This genetic information, as we call it, consists of a chemical substance called "deoxyribonucleic acid"—a long term, which is why you can refer to it simply as "DNA," as doctors do.

DNA looks something like two spiral staircases intertwined with each other, but each is so tiny that you can see them only with the help of X rays.

In order to build other parts of the cell—the machines I talked about earlier—the spiral staircases open, and single parts of the DNA are duplicated, as if they were being photocopied. The chemical process that allows this to happen is incredibly complicated. You need to remember only that these duplicates, or copies, leave the innermost part of the cell nucleus, and once outside, they determine, like a blueprint, which amino acids, and how many, are going to be built into a protein. Imagine amino acids as the letters of the alphabet from which you can construct different words. When amino acids (letters) combine, they make proteins (words, sentences, pages, books). Proteins are there to get the work of the cells done. By the way, a single cell contains about one billion proteins—a real mishmash of plans and commands, you might think. Still, every single protein knows exactly what it's there for and what it's supposed to do.

Günter Blobel

As in a factory, each protein in a cell has its designated location. Just picture an automobile manufacturing plant. Most of the proteins work together, forming the machines. Others are on conveyor belts and are constantly being worked on by the machines (like cars being worked on) until they are completed. Of course, there is no real conveyor belt in a cell. But there are many little compartments where the proteins are worked on, one after the other. To make this happen, it is extremely important that all machines be at their proper location. My colleagues and I at Rockefeller University in New York City discovered that all proteins have a chemical address that enables them to find their location. It's pasted on their heads and leads them to the right place, like the zip code on a letter. The doors to the compartments open only if the secret chemical code of numbers (the zip code) matches. Other proteins aren't supposed to sneak in through the entryway; otherwise, there would be huge chaos.

Why this big to-do? Here's why: Because not only do the machines in the cells have to work together, but all the cells in the same body have to as well. The cells can team up with other cells only if everything inside that cell works as planned. The proteins created on the conveyor belt by the "machine" cells—you remember these—assist in this process. Some of them get ejected from the cell once they are done. But don't think that they're now out of work! On the contrary, most of their work is only starting. They travel through the body, like messengers, making contact with other cells. An example: If you are in pain, one cell radios the other what it's supposed to do. And the ejected proteins assist in this task.

Maybe you once pricked your finger with a needle. When you do, the nerve cells in the skin at the point of injury send a message to the brain: "Ouch!" Instantly, the brain cells send back several messages to the body, making your hand automatically jerk back and causing your blood vessels to bring blood-clotting substances to the wound. In addition, white blood cells mobilize to fight any intruders, such as dirt. All these tasks are accomplished by the cells and their helpers, the proteins. Whatever happens in your finger is the same for all people, be it a fakir or you.

So why can the fakir sit on a board of nails without screaming his head off? The answer: He's able to suppress his pain better than you or I, or even to tune it out completely. How he does this, we don't yet really understand. One possibility is that he intercepts the pain messages from his nerve cells before they reach the brain and trigger the "ouch" feeling. To do this, he needs special substances that block these pain messages and suppress their further transmission. These substances are very small proteins that work the same way as morphine or similar painkillers. Since they do not come from a drugstore but are produced *inside* the body, we call them "endorphins," since *endo* means "inside" in Greek. All people are capable of producing endorphins—as are fish, toads, birds, mammals, and all other vertebrates. To be able to mobilize huge amounts of them specifically to suppress pain, like the fakir, requires a special talent or lots of practice. So now you can see that in the case of pain—even when we suppress its perception—proteins are always produced in certain cells and are transported to their proper place in our bodies.

Once we understand how the cells function, we can treat or even cure illnesses. Take insulin, for example. Insulin is a substance produced by the body to determine the amount of sugar floating in the bloodstream. It is life threatening when there is too much or too little of it. People who suffer from this kind of problem are diabetic and need artificial insulin. Now that we know how cells produce and discharge this hormone, we can put cells to work in the lab producing it.

Unfortunately, we have not yet advanced that far with other illnesses. Cystic fibrosis is a congenital disease in which the lungs are filled with mucus and cannot cleanse themselves. Most cystic fibrosis patients never grow old, and many die when they are still as young as you are. A protein with a smudged zip code is responsible for this illness. It cannot find where it is supposed to go and remains stuck in the cell.

By the time you are grown, we will know much

more about the inner workings of cells and be able to cure many more illnesses. Maybe you yourself can help with this or investigate why some people are able to suppress pain. We don't yet know much about that, although we know that the ejected proteins play a role in this process too.

Now at least you understand that what we and the Indian fakirs and all other people share in common is much greater than all our differences. All life is related—including you and me. As long ago as the Middle Ages, St. Francis of Assisi addressed his animals as "Sister Snake" or "Brother Wolf," and he was right. They are just as much a part of us as our real brothers and sisters.

Günter Blobel was born on May 21, 1936. He was awarded the Nobel Prize for medicine in 1999 for his discovery of the chemical formulas, or address labels, determining the movements of proteins inside cells. He conducts his research at Rockefeller University in New York City.

Why Is Pudding Soft and Stone Hard?

by Klaus von Klitzing

Mmmmmm . . . , you probably think when you slide a spoonful of pudding into your mouth. The delicious taste of vanilla spreads all over. All the way from the tip of your tongue down into your belly, you suddenly have this soothing-soft feeling—you don't even have to chew. It's a totally different matter, however, if while eating a plum you accidentally bite on the hard pit.

What is soft and what is hard—and why? These and similar questions keep us physicists occupied. We try to explain how such attributes of physical objects come about. The neat thing in all of this is that the whole world consists of only about one hundred different building blocks, including everything we see and sense. The differences among things—their color, their form, or their strength—depend on how these building blocks, which we call "elements," are put together. Just imagine the enormous multitude of life: people with different-colored skin, short grasses and high trees, insects, fish, birds, and mammals—yet the genetic makeup through which they all reproduce consists of these hundred building blocks combined over and over again in new ways. Hardly anybody knows that—ask your parents sometime.

Admittedly, you need an active imagination to be able to conceive of it. The Greek philosopher and mathematician Democritus was a most imaginative person. Twenty-four hundred years ago he had already declared that even the most different kinds of things were put together from the same building blocks. He was convinced that there must be an originating unit, a smallest piece. He called this piece *a-tomos;* translated, this means "not dividable." Since Democritus's atoms were invisible, and so remained unimaginable for most people, this theory was shelved indefinitely.

Not until two thousand years later, during the seventeenth century, did the famous English scientist Isaac Newton go in search of an explanation for why the Earth and the stars circle around one another in huge orbits. He calculated and calculated until he found equations that explained all the movements in the sky: That was the beginning of modern physics. His theory, unlike that of Democritus, could be confirmed because the stars are visible and you can therefore observe their appearance and disappearance. However, Newton was unable to look into the tiny building blocks of either a stone or a pudding. No more than Democritus did he anticipate that movements like those of the immense stars occur inside the tiniest objects.

Today, we know that an atom consists of a nucleus that is circled by electrons, the same way planets circle around the sun, or the moon circles around the Earth. The simplest element we know of, hydrogen, consists of only one electron circling around the nucleus of the atom. The addition of a single electron changes the character of the atom: its weight and its force of attraction to its neighbors. This is how the building blocks of nature are formed.

All substances that you know, including pudding and stones, consist of atoms. These join to form groups called "molecules." Depending on how the molecules are put together, different chemical substances are formed: fluids, gases, or solids—everything our world is made of. For the atoms, with their electrons, to come together at all, they have to be attracted to each other. Imagine two circus performers: When each juggles his balls by himself, the two acrobats are acting like separate atoms with their electrons flying about them. When they start throwing the balls to each other, though, you suddenly don't know anymore which ball belonged originally to which person, and both performers now have to do everything together. Physicists would say about this example that two atoms have combined to form a molecule with common electrons.

In a further step, molecules combine into larger and larger clumps. Depending on what they consist of, different substances form. Think of the pudding: When you stir the thickening agent into the milk, the fat and the protein of the milk combine with the starch of the thickening agent to form a "scaffold" of molecules, as physicists call it. While mixing, the liquid becomes thicker and thicker, since the many billions of atoms form new and stronger connections. Would you have imagined that with each spoonful, you are also eating many tiny orbiting electrons?

But why is my pudding soft? you want to know at last. Because its molecules are not very closely connected with one another and can easily separate again. Let your pudding sit out in the air for a few days and you'll see—what is left of the yummy stiff pudding is nothing but a watery, unappetizing heap.

Stones, on the other hand, are hard. After all, you

have to use force to destroy them—put them into corroding acid, for example, or alternate heating them to high temperatures, then freezing them. When you smash a stone, you can see its insides sparkle. Those are the atoms that have combined into strong and regular lattices that we call "crystals." Because the atoms in them attract one another so much, they move very closely together, and the billions of atoms form a regular pattern. The surfaces of crystals are often very smooth, and they sparkle in the light. If you have a microscope, just look at a grain of salt. That, too, is a crystal.

Luckily, we physicists do not have to smash stones every day. We can build our own crystals in the laboratory. In the process, structures are created that are so regular, they don't really exist in nature. Even diamonds are most often not purely white, but have a yellowish or bluish coloration. This is caused by tiny mistakes—for example, if the place where an atom is supposed to be remains empty or if the wrong type of atom has sneaked in. In the case of diamonds, the atoms hold on to each other very, very tightly, so this material is especially hard. If the same atoms hold on to one another in a different way, they automatically form other materials. The line drawn by a pencil, for instance, consists of the same atoms as a diamond, but its atoms hold on to each other loosely. That's why the atoms in lead can be easily rubbed off and leave a line on a piece of paper.

At the Max Planck Institute in Stuttgart, the place where I work, we prefer working with totally new materials that we invent ourselves. For example, we take three layers of one atom and five layers of another and build them up, like a ham and cheese sandwich, one on top of the other. You can play out all the possible combinations either on the computer or in reality, with very specialized equipment. The labs in which this is done have to be kept extremely clean so that no impurities develop. Where we are, even the air is filtered several times. Once a new material is made, we can observe its inner life with very special microscopes.

What would Democritus have given to be able to glance at the particles that he was certain existed, even though he had never seen them? For us, the riveting moment is when the material is lying under the microscope, ready to be tested. We begin to examine all kinds of things. What are the new characteristics of our material? Is it strong or fragile? Does it conduct electricity or not? Is it magnetic or not? Sometimes, we also want to solve a practical problem, like inventing a new tank for automobiles that would work with a fuel that does not produce air pollution.

So what does all this have to do with the pudding and the stone? More than you'd think! Just as stones can pile up on top of one another to form mountain ranges, we physicists can construct tiny landscapes from atoms. Some parts of these landscapes are designed to be hard and impenetrable, like a stone—or even better, like the edge of a bowl. Others are soft and flexible, like pudding in the bowl. This way, mountains are formed that will not let electrons pass or rivers are formed in which electrons flow especially well.

These landscapes of atoms are mounted onto microchips that steer electronic instruments. A single electron alone can work as a switch that you can turn on and off. You see, today, invisible atoms and electrons can do the work that in the past required huge machines. Isn't that fantastic? Many objects in your home work that way—your CD player as well as your washing machine.

Today's capacity for disassembling such landscapes and then putting them back together is called "nanotechnology." The Greek word *nano* means "nine." Imagine you cut a meter-long tape measure into ten equal parts. You would wind up with ten strips measuring one decimeter each—that is, ten centimeters. If you again cut each of these strips into ten, you get ten one-centimeter strips. The next division yields millimeters, and so on. If you do this nine times altogether, you have nanometers. This is how small you have to cut big objects, and how precisely you have to look, in order to understand the new materials that we produce.

And how these new materials are put together—more or less loosely or tightly—determines whether the new substance is as soft and quivering as pudding or as hard and immutable as stone.

Klaus von Klitzing was born on June 28, 1943, and received the Nobel Prize in physics in 1985 for his exploration of the quantum Hall effect, which has to do with the relation between electric and magnetic forces in nature. He teaches at the Max Planck Institute in Stuttgart, Germany.

What Is Politics?

by Shimon Peres

To answer this question, let's start by asking a different one: What happens when politics does not work? History gives us a clear but tough answer: When people cannot come to an agreement on their goals, sooner or later there's bloodshed. Instead of political debates, people fight with weapons—about land, about money and resources, or simply about whose voice will count in the future. Sometimes if politics fails, entire nations may come into conflict with one another when they clash over something about which they have different opinions: about their religious beliefs, for example, or about their ideas of how people should live in the future. People are capable of sacrificing everything—their own lives as well as the lives of others who block their way—for ideas they hold dear, if there is no negotiator between them. So the task of politics is to find solutions to complicated issues. And often, that means both sides must compromise. If that doesn't happen, things quickly become a matter of life or death, of war or peace.

Because bad politics turns so quickly into catastrophe, I especially care about building good politics. It's also important to me because in my homeland, Israel, the relationship to neighboring countries like Jordan, Syria, Lebanon, and Egypt and to the Palestinian people still very much depends on the question: How do we conduct politics in a way that avoids war? Although war is the result of wrong politics only in the worst case, you probably already see why politics is so important: Politics is supposed to create relationships among people and among countries, relationships that are supposed to be strong enough to allow for shared solutions even when conflict arises. Think of married couples. To live in harmony, each person in the marriage must think of the needs of the other. Sometimes they need to compromise. Sometimes each person must give up something he or she thinks is important in order to achieve the larger goal of keeping their relationship. Otherwise, divorce or even violence could ensue. It is the same way with countries, except the complications are much greater. Think of all the countries you know, where millions of different people live. It is hard to bring the wishes of so many under one roof.

That is why there are so many competing opinions to be found in politics. All politicians have their own vision of what the world should look like. Since they were voted into office because of this vision and their colleagues are pursuing their own goals, political conflict erupts over and over again. Things become especially complicated when the politicians come from different countries where people live and think differently. Yet they, too, must attempt to reach a mutual agreement.

It is not surprising that, despite these attempts, the political process often does not work—especially not here in the Middle East, where everything is more complicated, anyway, than where you are. Why is that? you ask. Because the three big religions—Judaism, Christianity, and Islam—originated here, where we live, and they play an incredibly important role in politics. Religions are such that, unfortunately, they allow for hardly any compromise. Each religion is convinced that it has found the only true path to human happiness. You cannot bear this point too strongly in mind: Where faith begins, reason ends. It is strange that while the similarities among the three religions are greater than the differences, even small differences can cause great hatred. Here in our homeland this is a very special problem, since there is nothing we need more in politics than reasonableness.

The influence of religion on politics also has positive aspects, for when people believe in God, they gain strength—strength to accomplish things together. The very same energy can have truly horrific consequences when one finds one's own version of God more important than all others. Nonetheless, I have hope for the future. I still believe that a time will come when wars are no longer fought over borders. I have this hope because I think that politics must work this way—with each people keeping its special character, its traditions, its faith, and its lifestyle, yet living peacefully with its neighbors. We need many good politicians so that we can achieve this goal.

You will ask: What is a good politician? Let's see: He or she should be well educated but, above all, curious. Being a specialist in a particular area is a condition. It is much more important that she or he knows how to bring smart and talented people onto the team. In the end, it is the leader that sets the goals and in the end makes the decisions, but he or she does not prepare for them alone or carry them out alone. The only way to be a good politician is to work with intelligent people who provide advice and prepare the work. For, you see, the tasks facing politicians are enormous.

We politicians are servants, advocates, ambassadors for entire peoples, in representative assemblies, administrations, in regard to other peoples or nations. We are servants of human dignity, human rights, and human values. We must always uphold the principle of equal rights for all human beings and safeguard their rights to be different, never forgetting the most basic right of all: the right to stay alive.

I know what I am talking about when I describe this responsibility—for more than fifty years, I have been active in the politics of Israel. When I look back, however, I realize how much politics has changed in these years. In the past, power still lay in the hands of politicians. Today, it more likely lies with the people themselves. In any case, a great deal of power resides with the mass media. By now every place where politics does business is wired with loudspeakers. Politicians meet in large rooms and do not talk directly to one another, but through microphones, while TV cameras record every movement and statement and transmit them to audiences across the globe. In today's world, the media often serves as a watchdog for politicians. But sometimes the media can be guilty of harsh and unjustified criticism. A good politician must be careful not to give in to popular opinion, but to stand by his principle. This can be very difficult.

Politics is the art of negotiation. We have to negotiate in more and more conflicts in faraway countries all over the world, countries for which we rightly feel responsible, because we do not want to have any more wars. We need specially trained and experienced politicians for this task, such as UN Ambassador Richard Holbrooke, the American who so successfully mediated the conflict in Bosnia. Dennis Ross, also a renowned ambassador, is an example of another American who has tried for a long time to bring about peace in the Middle East. Theirs is the hard task of creating contacts between enemies who do not talk with each other, but are ready to wage war. One thing above all is necessary to build bridges of understanding between hostile countries: patience. I know Holbrooke and Ross personally, and both of them have exactly this quality. They are very, very patient.

Perhaps no other kind of politician needs to better understand fellow beings or be better able to put oneself into another person's shoes as these highly gifted political negotiators. Although some of us politicians acquire new political abilities over time, we must not lose sight of one thing: The political process is losing more and more of its influence. Unfortunately, that's the way it is. If anything exerts a worldwide influence today, it is the economy. With their decisions, large corporations set the framework within which world history takes place. Nothing, not even the United Nations, which brings together practically all the countries in the world, can keep up with them.

Even if the influence of politics is weakening, it does not mean we can totally do without it. Just the opposite: We need the political process to mediate between rich and poor countries, to see to it that resources are distributed more fairly, to see to it that one day all human beings have an equal chance to achieve their life goals.

But let's go back once more to hot political conflicts. To prevent bloody crises, politicians should never give up their attempts to reach peaceful solutions. I want to explain this to you with the example of the Palestinian-Israeli conflict. To reduce it to the basic issue: There is only one country for two nations of people. Israelis and Palestinians fight over the same piece of land that, by the way, is just about as large as the state of Massachusetts. This big conflict is made more difficult because each of the two peoples believes differently in God (one Jewish, the other Muslim), speaks a different language (Hebrew, Arabic), and looks back upon a different history. Both peoples want the same for themselves: independence and security.

And what am I doing in the middle of all of this? I see it as my task to find a just political solution for this conflict. My idea runs like this: Full freedom for Palestinians, full security for Israelis. I believe that no real peace will be achieved until these wishes are completely fulfilled. You might ask, Why cannot Israelis and Palestinians simply live as one nation? Because it is too dangerous. Just look at Kosovo. Albanians and Serbs live there together in one country and yet cannot coexist. They take up arms against each other and try to conquer or expel the other even to this day. The situation in my homeland looks pretty similar, which is why it would be better if Israelis and Palestinians lived in two separate states with fixed borders.

To close, I would like to tell you how I myself became a politician. I was fourteen years old. At the time, Israel was not yet a state. I and many others were living in this undefined place in the Middle East with the memory of the horrors of the Holocaust, which had only recently happened to the Jewish people. The situation was dangerous, and we were living in a constant state of tension: At any moment we might be attacked by Arab armies many times the size of our own. The notion of a homeland for the Jews was being debated. I got my first lesson in politics when I joined the Working Youth movement. What I discovered was that the group was deeply divided. Some people were in favor of holding on to the entire land of Israel, at the risk of postponing the official establishment of the state of Israel. Others wanted a state of Israel immediately, even if this meant dividing the land between Jews and Arabs. This is when I learned my second and most important lesson: To win something you want, it is often necessary to compromise. If my grandchildren asked how they might one day become politicians of peace, I would tell them: "Always keep your eyes wide open. Do not be shocked by the misery and suffering you see. Realize that most people are too attached to their own memories; they look backward instead of forward. Only by looking to the future can you remake the world for the better. Certainly, you must not forget the past, but have the courage to have dreams, envision the world the way you most want to have it. For that, it's worth enduring all kinds of efforts. Be true to your ideals and do not be discouraged by defeats and setbacks, by moments of despair and anxiety. Do not be as small as yourself but as big as your hopes."

To end, I would tell my grandchildren: "People have a right to dream as much as they do to eat or drink. Set your imagination free, and you'll see that soon people look at you, sensing 'Here's someone who knows what he wants. Someone who's got an eye on the future!'"

Shimon Peres was born on August 15, 1923. For his political efforts in the Middle East, he received the Nobel Peace Prize in 1994, along with Yitzhak Rabin and Yasser Arafat. In 1997 he founded the Peres Institute for Peace and since then has devoted himself full-time to peacemaking in his homeland. In 2001–2002 he served as minister of foreign affairs and deputy prime minister of Israel.

Why Is the Sky Blue?

by Mario J. Molina

Snow white, lime green, lemon yellow: Some things make us think so much of a specific color that we simply name the color after them. Chocolate brown, ash gray, sky red . . . Wait, something's off. Of course, it should be sky blue! After all, the color blue belongs to the sky as obviously as black belongs with coal and red goes with blood. But why is the sky blue—at least during the day—and not, say, green or red? The more you think about it, the more new questions emerge: How can the sky be any color at all when it consists of nothing but air? Does air have a color? Does sunlight? And what is sunlight, after all, and what happens to it as it passes through the air? I want to explain all this to you in the way that we chemists and physicists think about it today.

People have been wondering about the color of the sky since a long time ago. Some thought that the sky was blue because the ocean was reflected in it. Others thought that it consisted of tiny little blue particles that were suspended in the air. And more than two thousand years ago the Greek philosopher Aristotle assumed that colors exist only in light, while the dark lacked all color. The wise Greek was right: Things around us appear colorful only because light falls on them. Although sunlight looks white, all colors are contained in it—red, orange, yellow, green, blue, violet (or purple). You can see these colors when the sun shines through rain and a rainbow appears as if by magic. This happens because the many little raindrops interrupt the path of the rays of light and force them to change direction. In the process, they push all the colors of the sunlight more or less off their course: Red light is deflected the least, orange light a little more, then yellow light, then green and blue light, while violet light is deflected farthest from its original path. That's why the colors in a rainbow always appear in the same sequence: red first, then orange, yellow, green, blue, and finally, violet.

But why do rays of light change their path when they encounter an obstacle? Picture the rays of light as if they were waves of water, and you've found the key to this puzzle. The Dutch physicist Christiaan Huygens had this idea 350 years ago. To this day, we scientists still believe that light behaves like a wave. Imagine a raindrop falling into a puddle of water. As soon as the drop hits the water, little waves begin to form and spread in all directions like growing circles. If these waves next hit a pebble or some other obstacle, they rebound and change direction. Something similar happens to light waves when they meet a raindrop or other obstacle on their way through the air—they are deflected from their original, straight path.

Just as there are small and large waves of water in

the ocean or in a puddle, waves of light also differ. What counts especially is what we call "wavelength," the distance between two peaks of waves. You can't make out the distances between the waves of light with your naked eye, because they are incredibly small—one hundred times smaller than the width of a single hair. However, the wavelengths of light can be determined very accurately with highly sensitive measuring devices. It then turns out that every shade of color has its own unchangeable wavelength. Violet and blue light have very short wavelengths, while red light, by contrast, has longer ones.

These different wavelengths are the reason some colors of light are more deflected by an obstacle than others. You can easily picture that, too, if you think once more about the pebble in the puddle: Small ripple waves created by a raindrop can be entirely messed up by a big obstacle like a stone. The stone, on the other hand, is a small obstacle for the kind of huge wave that you can set off with your hand at the edge of the puddle. That wave will simply splash over it and reach the opposite edge of the puddle without any problem. Something similar happens to the colors with their different wavelengths: The short waves of blue light are more easily disturbed by obstacles in the sky than the long waves of red. Now you know why a drop of water can scatter the white light of the sun into its many colors, which we then see in the form of a rainbow. In an instant you'll know as well why the sky is blue.

When sunlight shines from the sky, it always hits some obstacle or other—even when it's not raining. The air through which sunlight penetrates is not empty, but consists of many, many tiny particles. Most of them—ninety-nine out of one hundred—are either nitrogen or oxygen. The rest are other gaseous particles or tiny, so-called suspended particles that come from car emissions, from factory exhaust, forest fires, or volcano eruptions. Even the little particles of oxygen and nitrogen, though they are a million times smaller than raindrops, get in the way of the sunlight. The rays bounce off these many little "stumbling blocks" and change their course: They are being "dispersed," as we chemists and physicists term it.

As you can already guess, blue and violet light, with their short waves, become more dispersed than red or orange light, with their long waves. And that's the reason dispersed light contains nearly ten times as much violet light and six times as much blue light as does red light. Green, yellow, and orange light rays don't stand a chance against this predominance, so the dispersed light looks blue to us—sky blue.

The English physicist and Nobel laureate Lord Rayleigh discovered all this 130 years ago. To honor him, we call this process—by which light is scattered different distances from its original path according to the length of its waves—the "Rayleigh dispersion."

When you look up at the sky, you see mostly the blue of scattered light, not undispersed sunlight. That would appear as white light. You would have to look directly into the sun in order to see the undispersed light that comes down to you in a straight path—and you should not do that under any circumstances! Direct sunlight is so strong and so dangerous that, within moments, it can badly damage your eyes, and you can go blind if you look at it for too long.

You now know that white light can divide into all colors of the rainbow. The same is true, however, the other way around. You can experience this on a sunny day. Sometimes at the horizon, where the sky touches the Earth, the sky appears to be nearly white. At least, it looks a paler blue than the light shining directly overhead. The reason is that sunlight has to travel a much longer way to reach you from the horizon than when it travels from the center of the sky—and bumps against so many more particles in the air as it does so. These huge quantities of particles scatter the light several times, which is why it looks bluish white. By the way, milk is white for the same reason. Take a glass of water, place it against a dark background, and add a drop of milk. If you now shine a flashlight at it from one side, the ray looks bluish in the water. You are recognizing the Rayleigh dispersion. The more milk you add to the water, the whiter it gets. The particles of milk disperse the light more and more; white results. This is just what happens on the horizon.

The long distance from the horizon through the Earth's atmosphere to you not only makes the horizon appear lighter during the day than the sky directly overhead. At sunset it also makes the evening sky look red instead of blue. The many little particles that evening light encounters on its way to you scatter the violet and blue portion of the sunlight in all directions, until only a little bit is left for your eyes. So, you probably want to know now, Why can you still see the sunset's orange-red rays? Because only the long-waved orange-red colors can still reach you. The short-waved blue and violet rays are being scattered away from you. Why not observe a sunset? You'll see the rays that reach you directly through the air—which are, as you already know by now, mainly yellow, orange, and red. During the day, you mostly see the scattered light from the sun and the sky is blue; but at sunset you see the light that's not scattered and the sky looks red.

That's how we explain the red color of the setting sun and the blue color of the daytime sky. However, for some time after a sunset, the dome of the sky is still a deep blue. That is strange, because the few rays of the sunken sun that reach the outermost edge of the atmosphere should not only contain the blue of scattered light, but a portion of the other colors as well. It was only about fifty years ago that some physicists found the answer to this riddle: A special substance called "ozone," which accumulates in a thick layer twenty to thirty kilometers (around ten to twenty miles) above the surface of the Earth, is responsible for the blue color of dusk. This gas acts like a color filter for the setting sun: It absorbs the yellow- and orange-colored portions, but it allows the blue portions to pass nearly unhindered. Only when the last bit of light has died away do all colors disappear into the dark of night.

Ozone is not only responsible for the blue sky of twilight. In addition to the red and yellow portions of sunlight, it also swallows a special kind of ray that you cannot see: ultraviolet, or UV, light. I'm sure you've already heard how dangerous ultraviolet light is for all living creatures, including you. If your bare skin is exposed to it for too long, you get a sunburn. It's extremely important for all life on our planet that the ozone layer be thick enough everywhere so that it catches as many ultraviolet rays as possible.

Unfortunately, this protective layer, so essential for life, has already become thin at many places, and a huge hole has already formed above the South Pole. Certain substances that destroy the ozone are responsible for this hole in the ozone layer. Among them are what are called "propellant gases," used in aerosol spray cans to dispense hair spray or deodorants. My colleagues and I thoroughly researched one variety of substances that is especially damaging to the ozone layer. In the process, we learned how this variety destroys the ozone. Since then, this kind of "ozone killer" is not used anymore in many countries. This makes me hopeful that the ozone layer will recover again and that in the future it will continue to fulfill its important role of protecting life on Earth from deadly ultraviolet radiation.

By the way, it was living organisms themselves that created the Earth's ozone layer: bacteria, algae, and other plants, which originated the process of photosynthesis. My colleague Robert Huber will explain the process in more detail in the chapter "Why Are Leaves Green?" Here, you only need to know that it was the process of photosynthesis that began to fill up the atmosphere with little particles of oxygen. That's when ozone formed, since ozone is a form of oxygen. Nitrogen and "regular" oxygen make the sky appear blue during the day, while ozone colors the twilight blue.

The waters of the oceans that cover two thirds of the Earth also radiate blue. Though the continents in between are earth brown or forest green, the sky above is always blue—and not only as seen from our point of view. Even viewed from outer space, the Earth is surrounded by a delicate blue veil. The blue of the sky shines in the atmosphere. The astronauts who saw the Earth from above told us about it. There's a good reason the Earth is called "the blue planet." Its unique blue is the color of life.

Mario J. Molina was born on March 19, 1943. He received the Nobel Prize for chemistry in 1995, along with Paul Crutzen and Sherwood Rowland, for his work on gases that destroy the ozone layer. He teaches at the Massachusetts Institute of Technology in Cambridge, Massachusetts.

How Does the Telephone Work?

by Gerd Binnig

Do you already have a cell phone? One where you hear a soft beep when your friend sends you a little text message? Perhaps you even get solutions to math problems while you're taking a test. It's lucky your parents still haven't really understood how those short messages work! Otherwise, they would never allow you to take the thing to school. You can't even imagine life without a cell phone anymore. But do you actually know how the phone started? Why is it that you can call home from nearly every location—and how can your voice travel around the world and still be easy to understand?

When I was a child, cell phones did not exist. My

parents hardly ever allowed us kids to use their phone. They always said, "The telephone's only for emergencies," which is why we rigged up our own. We took two empty cans, connected them with a long string that we pulled tight, and there was our phone! Even words spoken softly could be heard well in the room next door if you held the cord taut and if you put your ear right next to the opening of the can. We were thrilled—it worked!

Alexander Graham Bell and his colleague Thomas Watson must have been similarly excited when they were able to talk to each other from two different rooms using the telephone they had invented. It was 1875, a time when your great-great-great-grandparents lived. For years, Bell conducted experiments until he succeeded in building what he called a "speaking telegraph." At the time people were already able to telegraph—"write at a distance," if you translate the Greek word into English. It was not, however, as perfect yet as a modern fax machine. A wire led to a device that had a disk with letters. When you turned a switch, electricity flowed through the wire. Depending on the amount of electricity, a needle pointed to different letters on the disk, which you could in turn write down and piece together into words. That was still pretty complicated.

The Morse code—named after the American who invented it, Samuel Morse—went quicker. Morse sent not dozens of different signals across the wire, but only two: short ones and long ones. Depending on the sequence in which they came, they represented different letters and words. The most famous signal is SOS, the international call for help among sailors: three times short, three times long, three times short. Morse's system is hardly ever used anymore today. Still, you might be familiar with the signal for SOS, for some wisecracks have programmed their cell phones in such a way that when it rings you get an SOS instead of the usual tone: *brr, brr, brr—brrrrr, brrrr, brrrr—brr, brr, brr.*

Alexander Bell, however, was not satisfied with Morse's signals; he wanted to transmit real spoken conversations. As a teacher of children with serious hearing impairments, he knew that words and sentences were produced by vibrations of the vocal cords and of the air we breathe. When he tried to teach a word to his students, he led the hand of the deaf child to his larynx so that the student could feel the different sounds and then be able to imitate them.

Vibrations of the voice automatically spread in the air in all directions at once—just like the circles of waves you see when you drop a stone into water. Sounds with different pitches produce waves of different size. To send the sounds from one destination to the other in a planned manner, Bell had to find a way to send the waves in one direction only, toward wherever the person was with whom he wanted to speak. In the case of the tin cans I told you about earlier, it was enough to have a string. When you talked into the tin can, the sounds caused the string to vibrate, and the vibrations traveled to the other can. However, we could not have called between, say, New York and Boston. This is because string consists of soft material and also because the air around it dampens the vibrations. Waves lose their power over long distances and at some point fade away.

So Bell tried transmission with electricity, just as he had when using Morse code. Electricity can also flow in waves—and much faster than the wave along a string. There are innumerable tiny little parts in an electrical wire, and they are incredibly agile: They are called "electrons." If you push some of them at one end of the wire, they pass along the pressure at lightning speed to the next ones, which transmit it in turn, and so on. It's like a crowded train in which one person bumps into another at one end, and this person, who's about to fall, bumps into his neighbor, and on and on. But electrons can do this without touching each other. They don't particularly like each other, and so they move out of each other's way. The reason there are so many electrons is because there are also so many protons around. Protons are located in the nuclei of atoms that the wire is made of, and electrons love protons. Now, if one electron gets too close to another one, it dodges it instantly. Electrons notice each other, because oddly enough, they, too, are constantly "on the phone" with each other. They telephone each other wirelessly by sending flashes of light, or photons. In principle, you could say that since electrons phone each other, we can too. They transmit the information along the wire, though I don't think they understand what they're transmitting.

Because electrons are so extremely light and because they can react so quickly, and also because they communicate through light signals, the pulse waves can spread as fast as light. Luckily, it works that fast; otherwise, we would not be able to telephone people on different continents. Imagine if we had to do that with the string! With luck, it would take, under the best circumstances, a full hour before one word arrived—if it arrived at all. What a boring conversation it would be! You would have to wait several hours for an answer.

But back to Bell: He kept tinkering with his contraption for a long time, but it generated nothing but screeches and whistles. The difficulty lay in transforming the vibrations of the voice into the electrical impulses formed by electrons. According to popular accounts, the long-awaited breakthrough came only by coincidence: Bell's assistant, Watson, had spilled some acid in the lab next door. In his distress he yelled, "Mr. Bell, come quickly!" Seconds later the door opened and Bell came hurrying in—he had heard his colleague, not through the wall, but through the experimental device that connected both rooms.

The long period of tinkering had paid off: The pattern of waves in Watson's cry for help had been transmitted to Bell's device by electrical wire. In order to turn the mishmash of electrical waves that had earlier produced nothing but whistles and screeches into something comprehensible, Bell improved his invention by stretching a thin hide—we call it a "membrane"—across the end of the mouthpiece. (Picture a piece of plastic wrap pulled tightly over a jar of freshly preserved jam.) This membrane caught the waves of Bell's sounds and transmitted them to a magnetic spool that transformed them into an electrical current.

Today, we call a device that transforms sounds into electric vibrations a "microphone." And we call the device that transforms electrical vibrations into sound—which we need, in turn, to be able to hear what was said—a "loudspeaker." It also has a membrane stretched over it. If you place your hand on it, you can feel the same kind of vibrations that Bell could feel from the throats of his students.

Bell founded a telephone company as early as 1877, to distribute his new invention all over the country. Phone lines were laid everywhere, transmitting conversations from one location to another, soon across all of the United States and Europe. Later on, huge cables were laid on the ocean floor that established connections between the continents as well.

Today, more and more people make phone calls with a wireless phone—the cell phone. It does not need to be wired anymore, because it works much like a radio: Cell towers broadcast the sounds through the air into all directions. Radio broadcasts can be heard by everyone who has a radio. The phone call with a cell phone, however, is aimed at only one receiver. In order for other people not to be able to listen in, the call can be decoded only by the phone with the correct telephone number. When your cell phone is switched on, it connects to a cell tower in your area. This station always knows where you are, even when you don't make phone calls, because your cell phone is always sending signals. You can't really hear them. Now, if somebody dials your phone number, the central station (the cell phone company) sends a message to all cell towers, but only the one in your area will react. It then transmits the call. And this is how the mess of waves in the air turns into a very special message, for you and you alone—the answer to the math problem, for example, that your friend who's sitting in the first row in class is sending to you in the back row.

Just as many people cannot talk at the same time

because no one would understand anyone else, in the same way you cannot have an unlimited number of cell towers sending signals, because they would interfere with one another. The space in the air for phone calls is limited, too. In order to save space, millions of wireless phones that now exist do not simply send calls in the form of waves, as do radios—they would soon get in one another's way and produce incomprehensible sounds. Instead, digital phones disassemble the speech and convert it into a digital code. It works something like Morse code works, with words disassembled into signals. Only in the case of digital phones, the signals are the numbers 0 and 1 instead of short tones or long tones—just as with computers. Millions of tightly compressed zeros and ones are broadcast from the cell tower or from a satellite at very short intervals: These are called "pulses." Tiny computer chips in the phones encode and decode the packets of numbers coming in and going out; they transform sounds into electronic signals or the other way around.

Maybe you've already heard about the new Universal Mobile Telephone System, or UMTS, that will be the basis of the next generation of personal cell phones. This technique not only converts speech into 0 and 1 signals and puts it back together again in no time, but it also converts music, text, or images. That is the reason why you do not just make phone calls with most cell phones, but also take and send pictures, listen to the radio, and surf the Internet. Soon we will be able to receive TV signals with them as well.

Many people don't even reach for the phone anymore when they want to contact somebody; they sit down at their computer instead. It has to be hooked up through a phone or cable line to the Internet, a huge worldwide network that connects some 200 million computers all over the world. If you have an Internet connection at home or at school, you can use it to send letters to Japan or to Alaska in seconds. This is e-mail, of course—the English abbreviation for "electronic mail." Quite a lot of computers can send and receive electronic signals and be connected that way through the air—the way you are connected today with your friends through cell phones. But wires will still exist nevertheless because they can transport such an incredible amount of information. They may no longer be electronic wires, but mainly "light wires," or fiber optics. We will then phone each other the way electrons do, with light; although unlike electrons, we will still need wires to do this.

It would be much more practical if we did not need instruments at all anymore, but could simply read minds. You think it's not possible? All right, it's difficult, for sure, but it's not totally impossible. Today, we are already working on tiny minicomputers with completely new kinds of chips. Chips are the tiny switchboards that today's computers need in order to do the computing. Instead, the new, fantastically tiny thinking machines may work with the smallest building blocks of our bodies, atoms. With these, we might be able to construct devices that work even faster than the fastest computers of today but that are nevertheless so small that we can build them directly into our bodies or our brains. That's where they would register our thoughts, convert them into electronic signals, and send them on to the receiver. Or would you rather not have anyone know your thoughts?

On the other hand, if these little thinking machines already existed, your friend could also beam the answer to the math problem to you, or the thinking machine could solve the problem directly. It will probably take a while until we get that far, certainly longer than you still have to go to school. But it's not simply a pipe dream of the future either—and if you're honest, isn't the cell phone already part of you?

Gerd Binnig was born on July 20, 1947. He received the Nobel Prize for physics in 1986, along with Heinrich Rohrer, for the invention of the scanning tunneling microscope. It is able to take very precise images of surfaces, which can go as far as to capture their atomic structure. He carries on his research at the IBM Research Lab in Rüschlikon, near Zürich, Switzerland.

Will I Soon Have a Clone?

by Eric Wieschaus

Picture this: You get up in the morning, late as usual, and you rush into the bathroom. But the door is locked. "Who's in there? Get out!" you shout, and bang against the wood with your fists. "Coming," says a voice from inside. The door opens, and who's in front of you—but you!

"I used your toothbrush. You don't mind, do you?" the other you says happily, and pushes past. "Excuse me, please. Got to go to school, it's already much too late!" And the you is gone. Can it be that you've suddenly seen a carbon copy of yourself standing in front of you? Looking exactly like you? With whom you could switch roles, as if you had a twin?

Well, for the time being I can assure you that *you* will be the only one using your toothbrush. Cloning—you can read about it in the newspaper or hear about it on TV—does not yet work with humans. "Cloning" is the name we give a technique by which a plant or a living creature is duplicated. No, it's not magic. It works—though in truth, not quite that simply. On July 5, 1996, a sheep named Dolly was born in Scotland. Dolly was the first exact copy of another female sheep, which had been born seven months earlier. Dolly did not have a father.

Now, you probably want to know how this is possible. To understand it, you first have to understand how you came about. An egg cell that your mother was carrying inside her body was fertilized by your father's sperm cell. That's how it happened: Your father sprayed a fluid into your mother's womb that contained thousands of little sperm, tiny creatures with long whipping tails. They engaged in a race to your mother's egg. The "winner" drilled his head into the soft membrane of the egg and dropped his tail, because it wasn't needed anymore for moving about. Once the sperm arrived inside the egg, the membrane of the head also dissolved, and its content, the nucleus of the sperm, was released. This sperm nucleus carried the genetic makeup of your father and, with it, all the information for the characteristics you received from him: the color of your eyes, perhaps, or your gift for language.

That you play the piano so well may have been inherited instead from your mother; the potential for it was contained in the nucleus of her egg. Both—the male sperm cell nucleus and the nucleus of your mother's egg—merged with each other, and in the process, the genetic materials mixed. Because both nuclei fused, the egg was fertilized. Next, this fertilized egg started to divide: First it turned into two cells, then four, then eight, and so on. After nine months you were big enough to leave your mother's womb, as a baby.

So that's how half of you came from your father and half from your mother. Despite this, you are a completely different person from either one of them, because their genetic material was mixed up again in a new way during fertilization. Sometimes it happens that you don't resemble them at all, but instead inherit the nose of your uncle Alfred or the hair color of your great-grandmother. You are related to all these people—which is to say, part of your genes match. Although you carry all these genetic tendencies within you, few of them become part of your being. Every human being is made up of roughly thirty thousand genes—something we have only recently learned—and everyone who is born is a new mixture of this genetic material. No human being is simply a copy of his or her mother or father. And no two human beings are alike.

But wait a minute. There is one exception. Sometimes, because of a quirk of nature, the embryo splits at the very beginning into two cell groups that do not stay together; rather, each grows into a full-fledged human being. Because these two people came from a single fertilized egg, they possess the same genetic material. We call them "identical twins." They not only look so much alike that you can confuse them, they also have the same preferences in music or food, colors or careers—even when they do not grow up together and are separated for decades.

Although identical twins resemble each other so much, they still grow to be different people. For, you see, at the time of their shared birth—as was true at yours—they are still far from having finished developing. They go on to play and to learn, they have different experiences with their parents and in school, they are lucky or have bad luck in life—and all of that has an influence on their personalities.

So what does all this have to do with cloning? A clone is somewhat similar to a twin, only a clone does not originate by chance from a fertilized egg, but rather in the laboratory, from a regular body cell. It is pretty complicated. All cells in the body originate from a single fertilized egg. That is why each cell of the body—whether a hair cell or a skin cell—has exactly the same genes. Why, then, do all the cells look different? Because in each cell only a part of the genes is activated. All the others lie dormant in the nucleus. Still, each of your cells contains the complete set of genes that you inherited from your father and mother.

Wait—there is one exception here, too: one's own egg cells (in the case of girls) or sperm cells (in the case of boys). These cells contain exactly half the number of genes contained in all the other cells of the body. It's good to know this, since if you want to have a child one day, you first have to see to it that an egg cell and a sperm cell merge into one, as you already know. In the process, the egg receives the second, missing half of genes—from the father, who has different genes. This is why the resulting child is never a carbon copy of his or her father or mother, but instead has a mixture of different characteristics, inherited from both parents.

Now, if you want to create a being that is completely the same as its mother (or father), and that looks the same, you can achieve this only through a trick. You have to take the genes from a completely normal body cell of the mother (or the father) and put them into an empty egg cell, one from which all its own genes have previously been removed. This egg cell is then able to develop into a new living being, even though it was never fertilized. Unlike the normal egg cell with its half set of genes, this manipulated egg cell has received a complete set of genes, even without being fertilized by a sperm nucleus. We call such a living being—the artificial copy of its mother (or father)—a "clone."

Dolly was such a clone. The first cloned sheep was not made up of genes, half from the mother and half from the father, as are you, but was rather a total copy of its mother. This is how it worked: The scientists took the gene-filled nucleus of a regular body cell. The cell was taken from the udder of Dolly's mother. They implanted this nucleus into an egg cell, extracted from another sheep, from which they had removed the nucleus. (They could also have taken an egg cell from Dolly's mother; the donor of the egg cell is not crucial.) Finally, the complete egg, with its contents exchanged, was implanted into the uterus of a third sheep. That's where it grew to become Dolly. So Dolly did not have a father. And Dolly was an exact duplicate of her mother!

But what is all this good for? you may by now ask. Why do researchers go through all the trouble to create a copy of a sheep? Don't we have enough sheep already? Scientists don't conduct cloning experiments in order to create doubles; they conduct such experiments because they want to find out, first of all, how living beings are really created. Why do completely different cells, organs, and body parts—arms and legs, eyes and hair, heart and kidneys—grow from a fertilized egg that has cells that are at first completely identical? Why do some people become tall, others small, some ill, others healthy, some bright, others less so? And why are frogs, fish, and mammals different from one another, even though they have so many genes in common?

We have not yet discovered the mysterious ways in which some genes are turned "on" and some are turned "off" and how, as a result, they fulfill different tasks in the body. Through experiments in cloning, we want to find out which genes are involved and how it all works. We carefully observe, for example, whether a clone does not differ from his or her mother after all.

To be honest, we have not yet discovered much. Although the birth of Dolly was a tremendous advancement, it does not look as if we will soon lift the veil of mystery about the way genes are turned "on" and "off." We are also a long way from being able to put endless numbers of cloned beings into this world. First of all, our methods aren't yet that effective, since far from every attempt has succeeded in cloning an animal. Before Dolly was born, researchers tried 247 times to clone a sheep, without any success. More problems arise when such cloned animals themselves have offspring: Cloned mice that are apparently healthy themselves have given birth to obese, ill babies. Possibly, the egg whose own nucleus has been removed is not really compatible with the alien nucleus—we just don't know.

Despite all this, we still want to continue with the research. It would be a great success if we could find out, for example, how diseases develop in the body. If we knew, for instance, why a cell starts to divide and eventually develops into a life-threatening cancer, we might be able to prevent it. Other serious illnesses like diabetes or kidney diseases might possibly be treated by cloning healthy body cells. For this reason, the British government passed a law several years ago that permits a special form of cloning: "therapeutic cloning." For this, not only egg cells from sheep and other animals, but also human egg cells, may be used in experiments. These special human egg cells, however, are not permitted to be implanted into the uterus of a woman, where they might grow into a living child, a new person. Instead, they are bred in the lab only until they have grown into a special tissue—for example, into heart cells or liver cells. Cloning researchers hope that down the road, complete organs can be grown with the help of such cells, organs that could then be exchanged with a diseased kidney or a wasted liver. This is what is meant by "stem cell" research.

You see, the special human cells, or stem cells, are allowed to grow only for a few days, after which they have to be destroyed. For all over the world, among people with totally different religious beliefs, it is still considered an unethical, forbidden interference with creation to make a complete human through cloning. Besides, it is still totally unclear whether it would work. Nevertheless, some scientists have already announced that they would like to assist in bringing cloned children into the world—on account of requests from men and women who are infertile but still would love to have their own offspring. Does this mean your parents could make a copy of you? Or that we could bring people who've been dead for a long time back to life, like the dinosaurs in *Jurassic Park*? Could we resurrect Alexander the Great or Hitler or John Lennon?

As of this writing, cloning human cells is forbidden in many countries. And we are far from having the technical wherewithal to do it yet. Still, it is just a matter of time until we will be able to clone human beings. Then, over the long run, it will no longer be possible to outlaw it. And when that time really comes, cloned people ought to have the same rights as all other people. Although genetically they will be the copy of another person, they will still be people in their own right. They would be their own people even more so than twins, if only because they have been born at a different point in time and have totally new experiences as a result.

Nonetheless, it probably gives you a queasy feeling to imagine that you might have a double one day. Do researchers like me have the right to conduct experiments like this in the first place? There is no easy answer to this question. I could say that we may perhaps gain valuable insights that will help us to cure illnesses. But I know that we're playing with fire here. We could make terrible mistakes if we clone some genetic traits because we're convinced they are especially valuable, and allow others to die out.

Nature has more foresight than we do. That is one reason why we have to preserve its multiplicity, the multitude of its genes. This multiplicity is responsible for different races, mentalities, cultures, and societies. Only because of our diversity has the human race been able to survive on this planet.

Professor Doctor Eric Wieschaus was born June 8, 1947. He was awarded the Nobel Prize for medicine in 1995, along with Edward B. Lewis and Christiane Nüsslein-Volhard, for the discovery of the role of several genes in *Drosophila melanogaster,* the fruit fly. He conducts his research in developmental biology at Princeton University.

Why Is There War?

by Desmond Tutu

I am a man of peace. How, you may ask, can a man of peace answer a question about war? Well, I believe that only when you truly know about war can you appreciate peace, so this is why I think I can tell you a little about this evil part of the human condition, this need for violence that makes us go to war with one another. I am also a man of the church, and my religious life has a lot to do with my thinking and my ideas for peace. War is such a complicated form of conflict, the ultimate form, so I will try to answer the question in several parts.

First of all, how does war start?

When two or more people disagree about

something, they argue about it, and each one tries to prove to the other that he is right. Sometimes they even hit one another. Maybe you have seen this; maybe you have experienced this yourself. If this argument involves many people on both sides, they might use different kinds of weapons to fight. Sometimes they use stones, or sometimes they use spears. Unfortunately, as people evolve, their weapons become more dangerous. Instead of using spears or stones, they will use guns and other weapons, which can kill the enemy from a safe distance. Then, the fighting can get so bad that people decide to use bombs. Nowadays they even have nuclear weapons, which are horribly destructive. So war happens when people cannot agree. One person says, "I am right," and the other says, "I am right," and they will decide who is right by whomever wins the war.

Now we can move on to the next part of the question: Why does a war start?

Although the people of the world live in a global village, it is sadly true that the people in it are basically fearful of one another. We eat the same cornflakes, we use the same computers, we see the same movies, and we belong to the same human race, whether we like it or not. In spite of these similarities we are afraid. Maybe it is because we are different colored, maybe it is because we speak different languages, or maybe it is because we celebrate God's existence in different ways.

Besides the basic fear people have of other people, there are many reasons why war will start. Sometimes it is because a very powerful country wants to bully another country. I am sure you have seen this behavior, or that you may have experienced it as well. The bully usually believes that the things other people have belong to him, or they should belong to him, and he will use some kind of force to take things if they aren't given to him. It is a sad trait of human nature that some people actually care to be aggressive. Within all of us is a very basic, mental urge that leads us to believe that using force will solve our problems.

And so it is with countries. One country may envy what another country has—it may have oil, or it may have gold, or it may have other valuable things, which can only be taken away by force.

Sometimes war can start because a country is worried that another country is oppressing its people. It says it wants to remove these oppressors, which is what happened with Iraq and the United States. The leader of Iraq was seen as a ruthless dictator who governed his people through fear. There were a few countries that also believed that the Iraqi leader had hidden very powerful, very dangerous weapons, which he could use to oppress even more people. So these countries decided to take away his leadership by going to war.

Unfortunately it is also possible that a war can be started by completely false reasons. Imagine a scenario where a powerful president wishes to hide a scandal, which is threatening his power in his own country. So he picks a fight with a potential, but not very dangerous, enemy. This kind of fight can escalate into a war while the scandal at home is forgotten. Lives are lost in the war, but the president has the chance to keep his power.

War can even start *within* a country. People may disagree because they belong to different ethnic groups or tribes, and sometimes they disagree so much that they feel they must fight one another. We call this type of conflict a civil war, or a tribal or ethnic war. On a historical note, almost every country in the world has had some sort of civil war in its past, including America.

And sometimes war starts because of injustice done by the government. This was the case in my country, South Africa, where a small group that was the minority of the people, the white people, gained ruling power in 1948. For years and years they used that power to oppress the majority of the people, who were black.

The black people were not allowed the same education as white people. They were not allowed to live in the same areas as white people, they were not allowed to be treated in the same hospitals as white people, and they were not allowed to vote for the country's government. White people had all the power and privileges. This system of government, which has become known all over the world as apartheid, an Afrikaans word meaning "to live separate from one another," went on for forty years. The black people tried to change that system peacefully.

But things did not change, and eventually, some of the black people decided to become involved in what they called an "armed struggle," which is just another name for war. Fortunately for us it ended in the early nineties when both sides decided it would be best if we became a democracy. We became a country where everybody, no matter what color they were, was free. Their dignity was recognized, and they could all share in the governing of their country.

I was not personally engaged in the armed struggle, but I know that during apartheid, the judgment of the world was that the struggle against apartheid was justifiable because the enemy broke the laws of humanity. The idea here is of a just war, a war that is termed as being morally correct. And that brings up another question. Is war ever acceptable? War is something that is evil, but a just war is seen by the world as less evil than the way things would be if you did *not* fight.

That does not mean that because you are conducting a just war you can behave in any way you wish. You have to abide by the conventions that the world has set up, which govern the way wars must be conducted. There was a group of world leaders who came together after the First World War, which went on between 1914 to 1918. They drew up guidelines of behavior for governments, and their armies, during wartime. These treaties were called the Geneva Convention. The Geneva Convention deals mainly with the rights of soldiers who are taken prisoner, as well as types of weapons one may use. For example, using poisonous gas or chemicals is looked upon as a crime, even during wartime, and after the war, other countries would have the right to send you to jail.

In the modern world, we have established a group of nations seen by the world as the legitimate authority when it comes to matters of fighting a just war. We call this group the United Nations. But it is very hard even for the United Nations to decide when it is moral or right to use force to settle a disagreement. The United Nations has established a set of conditions, which must be fulfilled before a war can be fought and be seen as justified.

The first condition is that the war must be approved by the United Nations. A country simply cannot wage war against another country for no real reason. That would make that war unjustifiable.

The second condition is whether or not a country or group has exhausted all the possible peaceful ways of solving the problem between the two sides.

The third condition involves the chances of success. Does the country or group have a reasonable expectation or hope that it will succeed? It is no use going to war if it is likely you will be defeated.

The fourth condition to wage a just war is that the means are proportional to the objective. That means that if you want to defeat a small country, you cannot use the kind of force you would use on a large country. The force that you use must be reasonable.

The last condition of a just war is whether or not the circumstances in the country are going to be better after the war than before it. If a war has been fought in order to liberate people, then it must be because their new freedom translates into having an improved lifestyle, such as having a supply of clean water, having electricity, being able to live in a decent home and to have a good job, being able to send children to school, and having accessible health care. The quality of life of the people must be enhanced and improved.

The purpose of all of these conditions is to make the war as humane as possible. After the war it is the goal of the United Nations to re-establish peace and stability in the region quickly, with the least amount of suffering. As you know from watching television, war is not just about bullets and bombs. Basic things like fresh water and fresh food, as well as clothing and medicines, are almost always a big problem for the people during wartime.

Speaking of TV, it is very important to understand the power of the media during wartime. It is difficult for people to know who they should believe during these times, even as an adult. I recommend that you sit with adults whom you trust and let them be the ones who guide you.

War is not a game. You probably know that, but it's worth repeating. I know that there are war games, which you can play on your computer or on your TV. You can be a soldier or a jet fighter–pilot; you can battle against an enemy; you can choose your weapons; and you can beat the others with a lot of explosions and, sometimes, a lot of blood. But the blood and the smoke are not real, and you can easily switch them off once you have destroyed the enemy with your smart moves and your intelligent weapons.

This is not the way it works in the real world. In the real world, real people die.

I am, as I said in the beginning, a man of the church, and it is therefore my duty to all churchgoers to help them seek good and shun evil. Ever since I started working I have tried to do this, and in the process I have learned quite a lot. There are some people who stop me and say, "Man of peace, man of the church, what do you say to the idea of 'an eye for an eye, and a tooth for a tooth'?" This was the old religious way of justice. I say to them that many people have made the mistake of thinking that the statement, in modern times, encourages revenge on every level. This is wrong.

The famous peace-loving Indian leader Mahatma Gandhi said, "An eye for an eye only ends up making the whole world blind." As a man of the church, I will go one step further here and remind you that Jesus says, "Love your enemy. Bless the one who curses you."

As we near the end of the discussion, we have to

ask ourselves if there are ever really any winners in a war. History has shown us the answer to this question. As a victor in a conflict, you may enjoy a certain period of terrific success. You think you have won, and you celebrate your victory, but you almost always leave someone feeling resentful. One day that someone might try to take revenge. We saw an example of this in Rwanda, Africa, in the nineties, where one group had oppressed another for many years, and one day the oppressed group took revenge. Almost half a million people were killed in the war that followed. Another example was in Kosovo, Yugoslavia. War may sometimes give the feeling that things have been resolved, but unless you deal with the resulting pain, resentment, and anger, the end of one war is really the preparation for the next one.

In South Africa we who were against apartheid discovered a better way to deal with our differences with others. We saw that fighting was not actually getting us anywhere. And so we decided to stop fighting, sit down, and talk with the enemy. If you listen to what your enemy is saying, and find ways to accommodate each other, you can end up finding, as we did in South Africa, that an enemy is actually a friend waiting to be made.

You may wonder why, as a Nobel Peace Prize winner, I am not able to stop wars from happening. Well, I promise you, I will keep trying. There are many Nobel Prize winners still alive and active, and they are all doing what they can to stop wars from starting, each in his or her own way.

I hope I have painted a picture for you of the elements that make up the worst part of our humanity, the act of war. But there is always hope for peace, because we still have God. God believes that one day there will be no more war. You see, the dream of God—yes, God dreams, too—is a dream of a lion sitting next to a lamb. And the dream of God is that we will turn our swords into plows and our spears into pruning scythes. We will take the things we have used for war and use them for cultivating the earth, for agriculture, for growing things. That is God's dream, and because God is God, that dream will one day come true.

Archbishop Desmond Tutu, born in 1931 in Klerksdrop, South Africa, received the Nobel Peace Prize in 1984 for his extraordinary contribution toward ending apartheid in South Africa. He is retired and lives in Cape Town, South Africa, but still participates in many issues concerning national and international interests.

Why Do Mom and Dad Have to Work?

by Reinhard Selten

Your parents have to earn money. You can see each time you go shopping with them what it is needed for. You pay money for all the things that you want but don't have. So you buy them. Everyone does that. If in school, for example, you want to have your friend's apple, you have to give her something else in return—say, a colored pencil or a marble. She gave you something, and in return she received something from you. We call that "barter."

Buying something is a bit like bartering. For instance, your mother goes to the bakery and exchanges $2.50 for a loaf of bread. Now, you may wonder why she doesn't simply give the baker a colored pencil or a marble. In the past that's how it was done. The fisherman paid with fish, the miller with flour, and the farmer with eggs or milk. Today, it's no longer common. After all, you don't know whether the baker wants to have a marble or a colored pencil. If he already has lots of colored pencils or marbles at home, he wouldn't want to give his bread away for that. He would say to your mother: "You've got to give me something else." And if your mom doesn't have anything else with her, she won't get any bread. Because bartering is so complicated, today we pay with money. The baker puts up signs that say how much you have to pay if you want to buy white bread or rye bread or whole wheat bread. The numbers written on the signs are the prices of the items. Everything you can buy has a price. Some things cost a lot of money—like houses or boats. Other things cost very little—say, a piece of gum or a pencil. It's obvious, isn't it, that a big ship is worth more than a pencil?

But you wanted to know why your parents have

to work. The answer sounds awful, but it's a fact of life: They keep needing new money—particularly on the first of each month. That's when they have to hand out money for an especially large number of things. They have to pay the rent or the mortgage for the apartment or the house in which you all live together. Your dad may have to make a payment on his car loan; it cost so much money, he wasn't able to pay for it all at once. So the car salesperson offered a deal where your dad pays a small amount every month until the car is paid off. By the way, that's one of the reasons you have to be extra careful when you're in the car and your ice-cream cone starts dripping—the car doesn't yet really belong to you. Part of it still belongs to the dealership or a bank, and you're supposed to be especially careful around other people's things. But that's beside the point. Many other things have to be paid for at the beginning of each month. The electricity, for example, which you need so the lights go on and the TV works. Or the water you use to take baths or cook noodles. Or the telephone you use to call your grandma. All of it costs money. Before you can spend all this money, you first have to earn it. Not all adults realize this, by the way, but let's ignore that. In any event, your parents have to go to work.

There are different kinds of work. Some people make things. We say they "produce" something. Everything in your home was produced by someone. For production, you need people. These people work in factories or workshops making something every day that later on you can buy. Now, you might say that people don't have to sell it; they could also give it away. Too bad, but it doesn't work that way. If you stand in front of a shopwindow and see a model train engine you'd love to have, you have to buy it—that is, pay money for it. Why this is so, I'm about to explain.

The wood for the model train engine grows in forests. Somebody has to go and cut the wood. He's paid money for this work. It's his job. Then, the tree has to be sawed into smaller pieces. That, too, costs money. Next, the wood is transported to the factory where the train engine is put together. The transportation again costs money: for the truck driver or the freight train. Finally, there are the workers in the factory who build the engine, who paint it, pack it, and send it to the toy store. All this costs money. So when the owner of the toy factory sells his wooden engines to the toy store, the money he receives has to pay for the wood and all the people who worked to make engines from the wood.

Imagine what an incredible number of wooden engines have to be sold to pay for all that! It takes a long time before the owner of the factory makes more money selling the wooden engines than he spends making them. When he earns more than he spends, adults say that he's making a "profit." If he spends too much money producing the wooden engines and earns too little selling them, adults say that he's making a "loss," because he's losing money. The toy producer has to watch closely that he does not pay too much money for the wood. He also has to watch out that not too many people work at making the wooden engines, because he has to pay all of them for their work. If he does not sell enough wooden engines, he does not take in enough money. He will run a loss and not be able to pay his employees anymore. Maybe he'll even have to let them go, and these unlucky people become unemployed. They no longer make any money and can't afford the rent or mortgage, or to pay for electricity and all their groceries. Most of the time, the government gives these people some money so they don't have to go hungry.

So the owner of the manufacturing plant has a lot of responsibility for everyone who works for him. He has to see to it that as many people as possible buy his model trains. If no one wants model trains anymore, he has to think up something new that children might want to have even more. There are so many incredibly great toys in the toy stores because the toy manufacturers are always coming up with something new for children.

In the toy factories, people don't just work to put

the toys together. Some people write invoices, or bills, for the toy stores. Other people write orders for the lumber suppliers. Someone has to organize how the workers work. And someone has to plan how to sell more model engines over the next year.

A long time ago people worked in fields or gardens—in agriculture. Farmers saw to it that everyone else had enough to eat. Later on, factories were built where things were manufactured with machines. As a result, many people no longer went to work in the fields, but in factories. Eventually, machines were invented that were able to operate other machines. Since then, only a few people have been needed in factories. Often these people only see to it that the machines work properly. Nowadays, more people are needed in offices. People work in offices everywhere. They think up advertising campaigns so that more people will hear about the wonderful model trains the toy manufacturer is selling. They think up ideas for new toys. They think about how model trains could be built for less cost so that profits would increase. All these people—your parents, too—get paid at the end of the month for their work.

The money is worth as much as the work they accomplished during the month. You know that from home. If you help to fold a sheet, you might get a piece of candy. If your older sister mows your neighbor's lawn, on the other hand, she may be given ten dollars. It's obvious, isn't it, that it did not take much time or effort to fold the sheet, but your sister needed nearly an hour to mow the lawn, and it was hard work. That's why she was paid more money for her work. It's similar in the office. Some people's work is not that difficult, and so they get paid less money than other people. Some people have a lot of responsibility—for example they look to see that the others did everything right—and so they get paid more money.

There are many terms for the money people earn. The money workers receive in factories is called "wages." The money employees in offices receive is called a "salary." However, you don't get this money in bills or coins. You receive the money in the form of a paycheck. This is how it works: The company your father works for has a bank account where the company's money is kept safe. Your parents have an account with a bank too. At the end of the month, a small amount of the money that the company owns is printed on a piece of paper—a paycheck. This is what your father is given at the end of the month. He can then deposit the paycheck into his account at his own bank. Now your parents can pay the rent or the mortgage and everything else. They can go to the bank and take out some money so they can go shopping. Most of the time, adults go to a cash machine; cash simply comes out of the bottom if they put in a special card up top and type in a code.

At the beginning of this essay I explained that everything you see in stores can be bought. You can also buy a toy factory or any other company that exists. You can own a company all by yourself, or it can be bought by a group of people, who often own more than one company. A company can also belong to a great many people. We call these people "shareholders." They have bought shares, also called "stocks," from the company. Such stocks are also known as "securities." A stock is a piece of paper that has its value printed on it, similar to a dollar bill or a pound note, and if you own such a piece of paper, you own a small part of the company. The more stocks a shareholder owns of a company, the more of that company belongs to her. If the company makes a profit, a small amount of this profit also belongs to the shareholder, because a small part of the company is hers, after all.

Why don't you ask your parents whether they own any stocks? Many people buy stocks from companies in the hope that the company will make lots of profits. If a company makes lots of profits, the value of each share increases. That is, the stock becomes more expensive as more people want to buy it. Let's assume that your dad bought shares of the toy factory and that the company sells a particularly large number of model trains in the following year. In that case, your dad could sell the stock for more money than he paid for it. Your dad will have made a small profit and be happy because he can buy something nice for you.

There are people who become very rich buying and selling stocks; that is, they have lots of money. Rich people are able to buy themselves nearly anything: a beautiful car or a castle or even an airplane. But not everything in the world is for sale. Some things you cannot buy. You cannot buy health or a long life, for example. Not even the richest man in the world can buy a chance to become two hundred years old. You can't buy love, either. Love exists for free—or not at all.

Reinhard Selten was born on October 5, 1930. He was awarded the Nobel Prize for economics in 1994, along with John Nash and John Harsanyi, for their pioneering analysis of "non-cooperative games," the situations where people cannot make binding agreements. He is professor emeritus at the University of Bonn in Germany.

What Is Air?

by Paul Crutzen

How long can you keep your head under water in the bathtub? My record is only about one minute. Well-trained professional divers can last somewhere between three and four minutes without breathing. That's the longest before they, too, have to come up for air. But why? Why do we constantly breathe air in and out, in and out? Why can't we simply hold our breath and be fine with that same amount of air for a few hours or days? If you know what air is, the answer is simple.

Air is a strange thing. You can't see it, you can't hold on to it, you can't even touch it. You feel it, though, for example, as wind blowing around your ears or as your own breath, flowing warmly out of you. Air is not firm like a rock or fluid like water. It consists, instead, of many different gases. One of them is oxygen—you probably already know that. Two hundred fifty years ago, however, not even the most knowledgeable people knew this. They thought that air was made of one single element, of only one kind of substance, like gold or silver. Then, driven by curiosity, they started to experiment. They mixed calcium with sulfuric acid until it fumed wildly. They dumped salt into soap solutions. They melted zinc and iron and tried all kinds of other things to learn what substances our world is made of. You'll experiment with similar things yourself in chemistry class, and if it's fun for you, you might have your own hobby lab at home.

It was also a kind of hobby lab where an Englishman named Joseph Priestley discovered oxygen around 230 years ago. Priestley was really a minister, but he fooled around with chemicals in his spare time. What would happen to various substances if you lit them? One of them, a red powder called "mercury oxide," lost its color as soon as Priestley held it to the flame. Simultaneously, a gas was formed that could be captured in a glass flask. This gas was oxygen. Priestley discovered that candles burned brighter and that charcoal glowed stronger if you blew "his" gas on to it. He also recognized that it was essential for life. He had placed a mouse inside a jar, added a small amount of oxygen, and closed it tightly with a lid. He then observed what happened and wrote it down in his notebook: "A full-grown mouse like this one would have survived for about fifteen minutes in regular air, my mouse however lived for one full hour." (Please don't try to replicate this experiment. Even a mouse likes to have a good, long life.)

Happily, Priestley later set free his experimental mouse, and it survived. If he had kept the little creature in the jar any longer, it would have suffocated inside, even though it could inhale air and had even received an extra portion of oxygen. Why? Because little by little, as he breathed, the mouse—you guessed it—used up all the oxygen. While the mouse breathed in, the oxygen flowed through his lungs into his bloodstream and, from there, into all parts of the body. We know today what happens inside the many little cells that make up the mouse's body—and yours, too: It's where oxygen is burned. (Without flames, however.) Another gas, carbon dioxide (CO_2), forms in the process. When you exhale, it streams out of your body into the air. So the exhaled air contains less oxygen and more carbon dioxide than the air you breathed in. Normally, enough fresh air is always around so that your lungs absorb enough oxygen with each new breath. But in an airtight room, you would have to breathe in again the previously exhaled air—air that contains less and less oxygen. Priestley's mouse had done exactly that, and that's why it nearly suffocated. For the same reason, you should never put a plastic bag over your head.

Candlelight also goes out if the candles don't

continuously get fresh air. You can easily see this for yourself: Light a tea candle and place an empty jar over it, upside down. After only a few seconds, the light will die out because every flame will burn only as long as it has oxygen—and enough wax or wood or similar fuel. Of course, wax and wood don't burn inside your body's cells, but bread and butter do, and fruit and vegetables, and anything else you've eaten and broken down in your stomach. If you haven't eaten for a long time, your body runs out of fuel and it needs new supplies. You notice when you get hungry.

You don't believe lots of little fires are burning in your body? It's really true. They don't have real flames. But they keep you warm and give you the energy you need to walk and to dive, to talk and to think. Without oxygen, these little fires could not burn and keep you alive. That's why you have to inhale new, fresh air to provide your body with new oxygen.

Besides humans and mice, all animals need oxygen to live. They all have to breathe, and when they do, they trade oxygen for carbon dioxide. Why, then, doesn't the air have less and less oxygen until none is left? Because green plants constantly provide new supplies—much, much more than they themselves use when they breathe. They succeed at doing this through photosynthesis, a process Professor Huber will explain in more detail in "Why Are Leaves Green?" Green plants catch sunlight in the green of their leaves, transform water and carbon dioxide into plant materials, and release oxygen. You see, it's thanks to green plants that there's always enough oxygen in the air.

Chemists have measured and determined that for every one hundred parts of air, nearly twenty-one parts consist of oxygen. Carbon dioxide, by comparison, is six hundred times less frequent. Carbon dioxide was discovered by the English doctor and botanist Daniel Rutherford, at about the same time as oxygen. Rutherford discovered yet another gas, nitrogen, that takes up the largest proportion of parts of air—seventy-eight in one hundred parts. Nitrogen does not change as it is breathed in and out. In addition to oxygen, carbon dioxide, and nitrogen, there are traces of several thousand other gases in the air. Helium, for example, which you pump into balloons to make them lighter than air so they rise by themselves. Or water vapors. They can fall out of the air again, in the form of rain.

Some of these other rare gases in the air contribute to climate changes and weather conditions. One of them is ozone, which you've surely already heard of. Ozone is a special kind of oxygen; it is formed from the regular oxygen in the air. Ozone is poisonous to plants and animals. Children can get a bad cough from it. Luckily, the air we breathe contains only one part of ozone in every ten to one hundred million other parts. Higher up, within ten to fifty kilometers (six to thirty miles) from the Earth's surface, the atmosphere contains about one hundred times more ozone—which is a good thing. Up there, the ozone particles block the path of the sun's dangerous ultraviolet (UV) rays, catching them before they can reach the Earth and make us sick. The ozone layer high above us works something like sunglasses with UV protection.

For some years the ozone layer has been thinning and holes have even formed. The guilty party is some special chemicals that do not exist in nature, but are man-made. They are called "chlorofluorocarbons," or CFCs, and they are used in aerosol spray cans and refrigerators. CFC gases are not dangerous in and of themselves. If released into the air, however, they are carried high up into the ozone layer. Together with other scientists including Professor Molina (who in an earlier chapter already explained to you why the sky is blue), I discovered what happens up in the atmosphere. Up there, the UV rays of the sun split the CFC gases into their component parts. Some of those component parts, in turn, help the ultraviolet light destroy one ozone molecule after another. During the spring of every year, all the ozone above Antarctica vanishes at a height of between twelve and twenty-two kilometers (seven to thirteen miles), and a great deal more of this dangerous UV radiation is able to reach the Earth through this "ozone hole."

As soon as we discovered this, we made our discovery public. Since then, fortunately, many countries have stopped producing CFC gases and have begun using other chemicals instead. Still, we will likely have to wait another fifty years before the ozone hole has disappeared and the ozone layer is thick enough again. That's how long it will take until the CFC gases that are in the atmosphere today will decompose.

Ozone not only serves as a protective layer against UV radiation, but it has a second important task: It helps keep the Earth warm. Together with carbon dioxide, water vapors, and a few other gases, it absorbs the heat that rises from the Earth to the sky and sends it back to the ground. It works a little like a greenhouse: Through the glass roof of the greenhouse, sunlight shines onto the flowers and vegetables planted by the gardener. Down on the ground, part of the light is transformed into heat or thermal waves that rise again. This heat cannot reexit through the glass roof, which is why the greenhouse heats up inside. Thus, even in winter, it's warm enough in the greenhouse to grow cucumbers and tomatoes. The whole Earth works something like a gigantic greenhouse. The sun shines through the atmosphere onto the Earth's surface, where some of the light is transformed into heat and rises again. Before this heat gets lost in space, it is intercepted by ozone, carbon dioxide, water vapors, and a few other gases like methane, and it is sent back down to the Earth. Since these gases work like the glass roof of a greenhouse, we call them "greenhouse gases." And what they do, we call the "greenhouse effect."

How fortunate that these greenhouse gases exist! Without them, the heat would dissipate in space and the Earth would ice over. However, too much of a good thing is unhealthy. And, in fact, year after year, huge amounts of greenhouse gases get released into the air, especially carbon dioxide and methane.

Humankind is responsible for this, since we use up more and more food and energy. Carbon dioxide forms and accumulates in the air whenever we burn any kind of gas—heating oil or gasoline, for example, when we heat our homes or drive our cars. CO_2 has also increased because we have cut down the huge rain forests, one after the other. All those trees are not available to use up the carbon dioxide in the air. Our craving for meat is also bad for the climate. There are today some one billion and three hundred million cattle scattered all over the world in meadows or stables, awaiting eventual slaughter. Methane bacteria live in the cows' bellies and help digest the grass that they have eaten. In the process, methane gas is created, which the cattle simply—pardon me—burp or fart into the air. And when the manure that's produced by all those cows, pigs, and other domestic animals decomposes, with the help of bacteria, methane gas is again released into the air.

There are several other reasons that greenhouse gases keep increasing, heating up the Earth. If this trend continues, then about one hundred years from now the Earth could be several degrees warmer than it is today. That doesn't sound like much, but it would be enough to melt ice from the glaciers at the North and South Poles. The runoff from the melting ice would fill up the oceans and flood many port cities and coastal regions. The climate would also change: Winters in northern Europe would no longer be so cold, and there would be more rain than snow. In some areas of the world there would be devastating floods, while in other areas droughts would dry up the fields and meadows. You get the idea: If we change the composition of the atmosphere too much, it could have disastrous consequences for us.

The atmosphere determines not only the kind of climate we'll have in one hundred years. Every day it also determines when, where, and how much it will rain or snow; whether it will be sunny or cloudy, warm or cold, stormy or without a breeze. Pay attention to the weather report next time you listen to the news: "A low-pressure system over the Great Lakes will bring humid but mild air to the mid-Atlantic, while cold air will remain over New England. . . ." Weather reports almost always talk about the air. These weather forecasts are very complicated. It's especially difficult to predict the weather for a specific location—even though it all follows just a few, simple rules. First, warm air is lighter than cold air. That's why warm air rises and cold air sinks. Second, warm and cold masses of air like to mix. That's why they move toward each other and create wind. Third, warm air is able to absorb more humidity than cold air. That's why it rains as soon as warm air cools down.

Pretty simple, right? Weather becomes complicated because the sun's rays don't warm the Earth evenly. It shines hottest in the tropics—so that's where warm, humid air forms. This air first rises, then moves toward colder countries, where it cools down and—you might say—shakes out all that water, as rain. What kind of weather happens on a specific day in a specific location depends on a whole slew of other things; whether it's summer or winter, for example, or whether the air masses, as they travel, can move swiftly across the oceans or become stuck on high mountains.

So air determines the weather, keeps the Earth warm, absorbs the dangerous ultraviolet radiation, and provides us with oxygen so we can breathe. We need air to live just as much as we need food or drink. And that's not all: Air is fun to play with, too! You can blow bubbles with gum or soap . . . pump up balloons, soccer balls, and inflatable boats . . . fly kites . . . make music with flutes and whistles . . . and blow air down the straw of your lemonade till it bubbles all over.

Paul Crutzen was born on December 3, 1933. Together with Mario J. Molina and Sherwood Rowland, he was awarded the Nobel Prize for chemistry in 1995 for work on the gases that are destroying the ozone layer. He is director of the Max Planck Institute for Chemistry in Mainz, Germany.

Why Do I Get Sick?

by George Vithoulkas

Your question sounds simple, dear child. But, in truth, it's another difficult one in this book, difficult for even adults to answer. The simplest answer would be to say that bad bacteria—organisms that get into our bodies through the air or through open skin—make us sick. I'm sure you've already heard this answer, from your teachers, your parents, or even from your pediatrician. In turn, you might have asked: If it is bacteria that, without exception, really make us all sick, then why didn't Dad get sick when Mom had a strep throat, swollen on account of streptococcus bacteria? Actually, we don't really know. Both your mom and dad sleep in the same bed and bacteria could move from one to the other without problem.

We medical doctors know only this: that people typically get ill when two things come together—an external agent that induces the illness (bacteria, a virus, a poison) in the person who gets ill, and an inner receptiveness, which is also called "predisposition." However, many doctors who were trained in modern medicine neglect the second aspect and concentrate only on the bacterial transmission of illness. They know that, usually, our bodies produce antibodies—a kind of police force in the bloodstream—that fight foreign agents in the blood. What they don't know is why some people who are ill often do not produce enough of these antibodies against specific bacteria or viruses.

The belief that illnesses are caused by bacteria may be one of the most widespread illusions of our times. All research builds on this belief. Scientists, medical doctors, and business executives sacrifice time, effort, and money for the battle against bacteria.

New bacteria-killing medicines are searched for, explored, and manufactured. Antibiotic medications make a good example of this focus. It's true that the patient who takes them for a bad cold recovers quickly from his cough. But the antibiotics not only fight off the cough bacteria. As a side effect, they can also weaken the immune system's ability to produce its own antibodiees to fight all kinds of bacteria from within, so the body can become more easily reinfected.

Many doctors argue that death rates have decreased significantly all over the world because of modern medicine. They mean fewer people die of illnesses that were still lethal about one hundred years ago. And this is true. Polio, for example, kills far fewer people these days. But if we look around, we see that other illnesses have increased tremendously. Alzheimer's disease—an illness that makes very old people forget everything, little by little—is spreading today almost like an epidemic. Millions of people suffer from it; recently, younger people are increasingly affected. It's not good when your sixty-five-year-old grandfather can't remember things. But it would be worse if the same loss struck your much younger father.

Illnesses never known before have emerged over the past twenty years. Perhaps you've heard of a classmate who has "ADD," the so-called attention deficit disorder, a totally new problem. These children are no longer able to concentrate. They always feel restless, they are anxious, they can't learn easily, and at times, they have trouble speaking.

So while it's true that fewer people are dying from diseases, it's also true that completely new syndromes of illness have emerged, ones that are more complex. Medical doctors who practice the very old science called homeopathy believe these two developments—the broader, successful use of antibiotics, and the appearance of new kinds of sickness—are closely related. Why? Because a truly healthy person can live a long, fulfilled life without once being ill. I have met people like that, isolated in the mountains of Caucasus, in central Asia. They live in the midst of nature, in out-of-the-way regions that suffer from little or no environmental pollution, away from new man-made poisons (chemicals sprayed on crops to kill insects, chemicals emitted from millions of aerosol cans, chemicals dumped into rivers by factories), which create new illnesses that did not exist in the past.

Most people today live in a dirty environment. We pollute the water, the soil, the animals; and then, through the fish, vegetables, and meat we eat, we pollute ourselves. Pollution brings disease. We get sick because our bodies grow more and more impure.

In homeopathic medicine, the idea is not to use medications to kill all the bad stuff in our bodies, the bacteria and environmental poisons. Homeopathic doctors believe that antibiotic and other chemically produced drugs only suppress the *symptoms* of the illness, but are not able to truly heal the deeper cause of the illness. Instead, homeopathic doctors aim to create conditions in the entire human organism that make it impossible for bacteria to settle in and multiply. In other words, we try to reduce the receptiveness of a patient to illness-causing bacteria.

It was a German doctor who first explored this path about two hundred years ago. His name was Samuel Hahnemann, and his medicines were effective in treating not only illnesses like the common cold, but also nonbacterial problems like back pain. More than one thousand homeopathic remedies exist. All of them are natural substances, like pulsatilla, belladonna, *Natrum muriaticum*, phosphorus, sulfur, mercury. In the correct amounts they strengthen the vitality of an ill person. For homeopaths always want to heal the whole person—body, soul, and spirit—not merely allay a symptom.

So if you ask a homeopath like me why people get sick, I first have to explain to you how I see health. Here is my homeopathic definition: Health is a person's total freedom on a physical, mental, and emotional level. By freedom in the physical, bodily realm, I mean lack of physical pain. A healthy body simply feels good. In the mental, spiritual realm, health means not being selfish; in other words, to think not only of oneself, one's friends, and one's family, but to be concerned as well for all fellow human beings. In the emotional realm, health means freedom from habits or ways of being that make us dependent on unhealthy substances or behaviors, such as smoking, gambling, the need to intimidate people, obsession with something. I mean any passion that interferes with being able to think and act in a clear and sober way.

Now, what does this have to say about the causes of disease? I'll give you an example: Our physical body becomes sick as soon as it takes in poisoned food. But people are fed not only by material nourishment. They also need mental and emotional nourishment. Poisoned emotions like hatred, jealousy, fear, and depression make us just as ill as do poisonous thoughts about how to steal things, to harm or even kill someone. These kinds of thoughts make us sick in our minds and, eventually, also in our bodies.

My own life has benefitted from homeopathy. I was a child of war, poorly fed, and lost both of my parents during the German occupation in World War II. I sold cigarettes in Athens to help me and my sister scrape by. The condition of my bone structure was terrible; one of the disks in my spine was damaged. After the war, doctors wanted to operate on me. Because an operation would have put me at risk of being paralyzed, I simply ran away. The pain stayed with me, but when I was twenty-seven, I came across a book by Hahnemann and learned how to heal myself. And I did: When I was fifteen, the doctors had given me only a few more years to live. Today, I am over seventy.

But back to the question. Emotional stress can weaken the body and make it vulnerable to illness. Under stress, whether it's emotional or physical, the human organism is much more susceptible to viruses, bacteria, and microbes. Here's an example. People who fly frequently breathe a lot of bad air—that's physical stress. That's why two to three days after you make a transatlantic flight, you might come down with a bad cold. Your body says: You treated me badly, and now I'm reacting!

Sometimes my body tells me the same thing and punishes me with the flu. Though I don't take antibiotics, I know that at my age to travel all that much is unhealthy. Why do I still do it, knowing how unhealthy stress is? Because, before I die, I want to convince the world of all the possibilities homeopathy offers. Because I've seen how many people can be healed by homeopathy.

Modern medicine is valuable and necessary, especially in cases of accidents and serious illnesses, like cancer. In my view, however, modern medicine does not have the proper means to regenerate, to truly heal a sick body. It takes care of the symptoms of disease—a fever or a headache, for example—without curing the body on a much deeper level.

In my view, we have to understand the mechanism of illnesses before we can truly heal them. No illness is simply what we notice in its final stages. Illness starts much earlier, in reaction to some imbalance in the body. It is an imbalance of energies, of "spirit" that comes out, over time, in a disturbance of one organ or another. If we really want to understand why we get sick, we have to learn to understand these energy disturbances on a spiritual level. We need to acquire an understanding of how and why poisonous thoughts and feelings influence the body. The ancient Greeks knew that this influence must be very strong, because already then they talked about the importance of a healthy mind on a healthy body.

If we lived in an ideal society, we'd probably all be much healthier and happier. If we want health for ourselves, we have to create a healthy society, too, in which we care as much about others as we do about ourselves. Instead, we fight wars and argue and compete with one another. We cannot get healthy as long as we are unable to stop our inner aggression and our negative attitudes toward fellow human beings, as long as we don't really behave as if we are all children of the same great creator.

Homeopathic healing begins here, at this source of illness. But our understanding has not grown as much as our ability to heal.

I don't know whether at some point I will be smart enough to find the definitive answer to your question. But I have the serious intention to try, in a book of my own.

George Vithoulkas was born on July 25, 1932. He was awarded the Right Livelihood Award, also known as the Alternative Nobel Prize, in 1996 for his success in spreading the knowledge of homeopathy. The Right Livelihood Award was founded in 1980 by Jacob von Uexküll in order to honor groups of people and individuals around the globe who have done outstanding work "on behalf of our planet and our people." Meant to counterbalance the official Nobel Prize, which von Uexküll saw as "oriented towards the political and scientific establishment of the Western world," the

Alternative Nobel Prize exists to strengthen the positive social forces its recipients represent. At an annual ceremony in Stockholm in the Swedish Parliament, the presentation of the award takes place in December, usually on the day before the Nobel Prize ceremony.

Vithoulkas used his prize money to establish an academy on the Greek island of Alónnisos, which also offers educational programs for modern medical doctors from all over the world.

Why Are Leaves Green?

by Robert Huber

Are you looking forward to spring already, when nature becomes colorful again? The lilacs light up with purple; the dandelions, yellow; and the first poppies, red. Only the leaves on the trees are green—green and nothing but green. Why don't they join the color competition? Well, they have better things to do, and they need their green for it.

This green substance in leaves is called "chlorophyll," and it ensures that trees survive and grow and that new trees rise from the ground—all without their having to eat another creature. Chlorophyll is able to do something no color of blossoms can do. It converts sunlight into electrical current that is used to transform air and water—nothing more—into sugar. "Photosynthesis" is what we chemists call this magic; the word is Greek in origin, and it means "to put together with light." Green plants later combine the sugar with other nutrients they extract from the soil, and with it, they build new leaves, blossoms, and fruit.

For you to understand how photosynthesis works, I first have to tell you something about light. Sunlight is full of colors. If you don't believe me, just take a hose and aim the water right into the sun. You'll see the many colors of light, one right next to the other. The light separates inside the little drops of water and paints a small rainbow in the air: Red is outside, then orange, yellow, green, blue, and all the way inside it's purple—just the way it is in a huge rainbow in the sky. (Please see Professor Molina's essay, "Why Is the Sky Blue?" in this book for more information about color and light.)

Usually, you see all the colors of light at the same time, and so they appear colorless. As soon as one of the colors is missing, you see a mixture of the remaining ones. When all colors are gone, things look as black as night. When only one color is left, that's the color you see. Dandelions are yellow because they absorb all the colors of sunlight except yellow. Tinky Winky on the TV show *Teletubbies* is purple because its fur absorbs all colors but purple. Leaves are green because they let all colors of the light disappear except green.

Therefore, we see only the color an object leaves visible to our eyes. But what happens to the other colors? They are transformed, usually into heat. Think of the use of infrared lamps in bathrooms to quickly warm them up. Violet light is especially hot, as is ultraviolet, or UV, light. This hot UV light—invisible to your eyes, by the way—is responsible for the sunburn you get when you have had too much sun.

I'm sure that now you want to know how colored light changes into heat. Well, picture the sun as a clown, constantly juggling red, yellow, green, and blue balls. We scientists call these balls "photons."

Now go on to imagine that all existing things—say, flowers, cars, clothes, or your skin—are filled with little seesaws: One end of each seesaw is empty, and on the other is a golf ball. All the golf balls—we call them "electrons"—jump up into the air once the clown throws a ball, a photon, onto the empty side of the seesaw. And whenever an electron drops down again, it gives off a little heat.

Obviously, there are no little seesaws inside dandelions or Tinky Winky's fur. But electrons really do exist. They are inside everything. As soon as light shines on them and hits them with photons, they jump up and down. While they're coming back down, the electrons always produce a little bit of thermal energy. The green substance in the leaves, containing chlorophyll, manages to convert this energy into electrical current—just like a tiny generating plant! This is the reason it's so important that plants have leaves that are green and not, say, pink or blue. The green chlorophyll makes sure that the electrons stirred up by the light don't drop down again and waste all the heat. Instead, little particles of green chlorophyll throw the electrons next door. The neighbor catches them and, in turn, passes them along, until they reach the place where they're needed. This keeps working only as long as there's light, but it happens at a speed we can't imagine, one trillion times faster than a second. The electricity generated in the process is nothing to worry about—it's not at all dangerous, you can't even feel it.

To make sure that this electricity does not get lost again, it is passed along a kind of wall to the innermost part of the leaf. Chlorophyll is mounted alongside this wall and contributes to making this passageway. On the other end of the wall, chemical substances receive the electrical energy and turn it into a new substance called adenosine triphosphate, or "ATP." This substance is extremely important because it stores the energy like coins in a treasure chest, until the leaves need it. Let's assume that somebody gives you eggs, milk, and flour. I'm sure you know how to make pancakes from them: First mix them all up with an electric beater, then cook the batter in a pan until it's crisp and brown. To do this, you need electricity for the beater and electricity or gas for the stove-top burner. It's like that with leaves as well. They can get air and water all for free from nature, and they know how to make it into valuable sugars. But they need energy to combine these ingredients—and the ATP delivers the energy.

How do I know all of this? If you look at a leaf through a magnifying glass, you see veins, grooves, and bumps, but you don't see the tiny electrons and the green particles with the chlorophyll. To see these, you need a special microscope that makes everything look ten million times larger. If you were able to enlarge a soccer ball that much, it would be almost as big as all of Montana or California. Some fifteen years ago my colleagues and I saw these tiny chlorophyll particles with the help of such a supermicroscope, which uses X rays, and we also discovered the path of the electrons. Well, not quite. We did not really explore leaves, but bacteria that can also carry out photosynthesis in a way similar to leaves.

You and I also need large amounts of sugar in order to live, as well as proteins and fats. But because we do not have chlorophyll to turn the sun's energy into ATP, we have to get all our important substances from food: from fruit and salad, nuts, and other parts of plants. Or from the meat of animals that had previously fed on plants. Notice right away that we can't do without plants. Without them, animals and people would simply starve to death—and we'd suffocate, to boot, since the oxygen that sustains life also comes from plants. During photosynthesis, plants make oxygen from water as a byproduct and release it into the air.

When we breathe, oxygen is taken up by the lungs and is distributed in the blood throughout the body. Your body needs oxygen. Everything you eat is converted to energy with the help of oxygen: energy to play soccer, to ride your bike, to think. Your brain needs especially large amounts of energy.

Maybe you now wish that humans, too, had this

wonderful chlorophyll so that we could make sugars and oxygen ourselves. Unfortunately, that wouldn't be a good idea. If you were to inject chlorophyll under your skin, you would become so sick that you might die. Chlorophyll by itself, without the wall on which it's mounted and without ATP, is extremely dangerous. It throws off electrons, as I explained earlier, and then it doesn't know what to do with them. Soon electrons would be swarming all over your body, wrecking everything around them and seriously harming you.

By the way, too many electrons gone wild can also wreak havoc in healthy green leaves. If the sun is especially hot, for example, the chlorophyll cannot process that much solar energy fast enough. Unfortunately, trees cannot protect themselves from the sun the way we can. That's when red- , yellow- , and orange-colored substances step in. They simply make the many extra electrons drop back down to where they were, so that the energy dissipates as heat and does not cause any damage.

Robert Huber

These colorful "lightning rods" are inside the leaves all summer long, but their colors are concealed by all the green particles of chlorophyll. They are especially important in the fall. You see, before a tree drops its leaves, the valuable green stuff is transformed into all kinds of other substances and stored as supplies for the following year. When all the green finally disappears from the leaves, the other colors become visible, which is why trees in the fall light up with such brilliant yellows, oranges, and reds.

Robert Huber was born on February 20, 1937. He was awarded the Nobel Prize for chemistry in 1988, along with Johann Deisenhofer and Hartmut Michel, for establishing the three-dimensional structure of a "photosynthetic reaction center." He conducts his research at the Max Planck Institute for Biochemistry in Martinsried, near Munich, and teaches at the Technical University of Munich in Germany.

Why Do I Forget Some Things and Not Others?

by Erwin Neher

What was for dinner last night? You don't remember? Well. It's not that important. Where can you find the brakes on your bicycle? I'm sure you remember that, right? No doubt you remember to go when the light is green and not red. Whoever forgets something that important may easily find himself run over.

By the way, prehistoric men already had to cope with this danger, even though they had no cars and traffic lights. They needed to remember other things instead, things that were important in their lives—which berries were edible, for example, or how to keep safe from lions. Whoever failed to learn this in time and fix it in his or her mind simply starved to death or was eaten alive. The only people who survived were those who could tell apart the important from the unimportant and those who remembered particularly well what was most important. The rest simply died off, along with their life-threatening forgetfulness. In this way, people have been trained to remember what is important, and to forget what isn't, over the many millions of years of their existence.

Some things are important for everyone—to know the traffic rules, for instance, or to know the difference between regular ivy and poison ivy. Other things may be of interest only to you, like the name of the nice kid at the party or when the video store with all your favorite games is open. How much you remember from English class depends on what else is going on in your head. It also matters whether you enjoy learning. Things that leave you cold go in one ear and out the other. Things you want to learn often stick the first time around. You'll certainly memorize your Spanish vocabulary faster if you want to understand the words to your favorite Latin American song.

If you have trouble anyway with this word or that, you have to cram it in your brain again and again, until it sticks.

It's thanks to your brain that you remember anything at all. It consists of about one hundred billion nerve cells, also called "neurons," each of which is connected to more than one thousand others. Each nerve cell transmits very special messages—but only when they work with other neurons do they give you the ability to feel, move, think, learn, and remember things.

A neuron looks something like a crumpled ball with many short little branches and one long, protruding arm. It can receive messages from other nerve cells with its short little branches, and it can pass them along with its long arm. Lots of little fingers grow out of the long arm and messages jump from these fingers to the short little branches of nearby cells. Your nerves are made up of whole bundles of long arms. The auditory nerves, used for hearing, conduct sounds and noise from your ears to your brain. Touch-sensitive nerves transmit sensations of touch. And the optical nerves transmit visual images. After passing through many relay stations, each kind of impression arrives at a very specialized place in the brain: sounds and noise in the auditory center, touch in the center for body sensations.

All this sounds simple, but it's really pretty complicated. For example, more than one hundred million nerve cells are busy while you're looking at a cartoon elephant on the TV screen. Each of those cells is focused on but one tiny little part of the elephant. Some get stimulated only by his blue color and respond to no other stimuli; others are stimulated only by the black and white of the elephant's eyes. Some nerve cells react only to the vertical lines that depict his legs, others to the horizontal line that defines his back. Still others become active only once the elephant moves. There are even specialized neurons that perceive rounded shapes and angular edges. Each of them responds only when it recognizes something for which it is specialized, and then it forwards the signal to more deeply lying regions in the brain. There, all the messages that arrive at the same time are put together like a puzzle. That's why you don't see the elephant in single parts, but rather as one whole, the way it was drawn. For you to be able to recognize this blue thing as an animal in an animated cartoon, more than thirty brain regions specializing in vision have to cooperate with several other regions that are scattered widely all over the brain.

Auditory nerves work in a similar way when the elephant trumpets or the blinking eyes of a cartoon mouse go *clink.* Some nerve cells transmit only low sounds, others high and very high ones. These single messages get reintegrated in the auditory or hearing center into trumpeting or clinking. But that's not all: The auditory and visual centers are in a continuous interchange with each other and other regions of your brain; they form a real network of neural connections. That's why you can see the mouse and the elephant, hear your own laughter, and smell dinner being cooked in the kitchen all at the same time. A formation lies deep inside your brain and is hooked in with all the centers and is constantly exchanging information with them. This formation, shaped like a little sea horse, is about as big as your thumb and is called the "hippocampus," which is Greek for "sea horse."

If you watch your cartoon show often, you know that they do not always run a new cartoon episode; some are repeated every once in a while. When it's a rerun—that is, when you see the same episode a second time—the same nerve cells are stimulated as they were the first time, and they transmit the messages across similar pathways to the brain. The more often the same "networks of neurons" are used, the more tightly they interlace: Neurons simply stretch more of their fingers out to their neighboring neurons and transmit the messages faster. If the cells in the network of neurons are connected tightly enough, the hippocampus succeeds in learning and remembering this network. Next time around, something flashes through your head: *Boy, that's familiar—I've seen this before!* You recall this specific cartoon episode; it stayed in your memory.

It's easy to prove that the hippocampus plays an important role in all this. When this area of the brain has been destroyed due to an illness or accident, the person can no longer remember anything new. Such people are in no way stupid, but they always forget what month it is or what their new neighbor's name is. On the other hand, they can remember lots of experiences from their childhoods. Memory for things long past is not located in the hippocampus, but elsewhere in the brain.

Today, we brain researchers have the following picture: The hippocampus stores your memories for a certain time, then passes them on to other regions of the brain located more closely to your skull—the cortex. We don't exactly know how they get there. In any case, some of them are stored there throughout your life. This long-term storage, however, does not work like the data storage in your computer. A computer stores each unit of information at a very specific place on your hard drive. It is entered there for good, like the numbers in a phone book. A computer doesn't forget anything, unless it crashes. If you recall stored data onto your screen, it appears in exactly the same way in which you saved it.

Your brain works differently. It does not store whatever you experienced or learned in a specific place in the hippocampus or the cortex. Instead, it works this way: The more often you see, hear, and, if studying, try to memorize the same thing, the stronger become the connections among the optical and auditory nerves and all other neurons involved in seeing, hearing, and studying. So when you now remember what you saw, heard, and learned, you get roughly the same messages running through this strong network of neurons as those that were running earlier during seeing, hearing, and learning—though your eyes and ears are not at all involved this time around. The information that originally came from your sensory organs is supplemented by "brain storage," and something is added to it in the delivery. Each time you remember something, intentionally or unintentionally, the already strong neural pathways and their connections get a little stronger—all the more so the more important something is.

You can picture this tangle of neural networks like doodles scribbled all over a piece of notepaper. How quickly it fills up—say, during phone calls—with all kinds of words and drawings! Important information, like the time and place of a birthday party or the address of your new friend, winds up on it just as easily as meaningless doodles that you scrawled while lost in thought. You might retrace the important notes, perhaps with extra-thick lines that cover all the other stuff, before they get lost in the mass of unimportant scribblings. Doing so, you might once make a mistake while retracing the date of the party or something else important. Or it might be that each time you meet your friend, you think of the silly stick figure you accidentally doodled next to her address. Something of the same sort that happens with the scribbled-on notepaper also happens with your memory. Sometimes when you think back on something, little mistakes or inexactitudes sneak in. Or a specific experience triggers the memory of something completely different that happened at the same time.

Maybe you were eating ice cream when you first heard your favorite song on the radio, and now that melody runs through your head whenever you have ice cream. In your brain, these two events are connected once and for all, and you won't easily forget them. Just as a spiderweb trembles as a whole when you touch one part of it, so the whole network of neurons gets excited when only one part of the neural pathways transmits messages. Initially, the hippocampus is responsible for this effect. Later on it's the cortex that's doing it. You can take advantage of it when you're studying: If you have trouble remembering something, think of something you've already known for a long time and that you know you won't forget. Using this memory trick, or "mnemonic device," you can remember the weird-sounding names of cities you have to learn for geography class. Impressions or experiences that made you very happy, sad, angry, or anxious stick with you with special clarity and for a long time. If, for example, you once survived a night in a mountain hut shivering under your covers because of a terrible surprise thunderstorm, you would still remember your queasy feelings again many years later if you spent another night in the same hut. Such strong interconnectedness between experiences and feelings is created by a region in the brain located right next to the hippocampus. It is about the size of a walnut, and it is called "amygdala," which means "almond-shaped" in Greek.

You now know that your brain has many regions that take on special tasks. I've already mentioned the auditory and optical centers, the hippocampus and amygdala. There are also many regions, especially in one part of the cortex, about whose functions little is yet known. But this much is certain: You need them in order to find your way around unfamiliar territory or among strangers, to solve problems, and to make plans. Only with the help of these regions can you bring about the complex achievements that distinguish human beings from less intelligent life. In fact, these regions of the cortex take up almost twice as much space in your brain as they do in a chimpanzee's and ten times as much as in a cat's. Worms and flies do not have a cortex at all, because their nervous system is built in a completely different way. Still, they, too, are equipped to differentiate between the important and unimportant and to remember what is important. Every caterpillar knows even before it hatches which leaves are edible. And every earthworm knows it must hide from too strong a sun. If it didn't, it would not survive. Caterpillars and earthworms can even learn simple things and remember them for a short while. Tickle a worm with a blade of grass, and it will retract its head. If you do this repeatedly, it will soon stop reacting—it has learned that the blade of grass doesn't do anything really bad. Each time it was tickled, its neurons formed more little branches that strengthened the connections and sent on more quickly the message: Something's tickling me, but nothing else happens.

So an earthworm's nerve cells work the same as the nerve cells in your body. The only difference is that your brain is capable of building many more nerve networks that intertwine in a complicated way. The older you get and the more you experience and learn, the more diversified the connections among your neurons become—many of them are formed to last. As a newborn baby, you already had almost as many neurons as you will have as an adult. By far, not all their connections, however, were developed yet. Many important connections are formed only weeks or years after your birth. Some neural pathways can form only if they are stimulated at the right time. If someone had covered one of your eyes with a patch for two weeks right after you were born, you would have been blind forever in that eye, even though it was totally healthy! If the optical nerves responsible for vision are not stimulated during this critical time period, they cannot develop any connections to the optical brain center. The brain adapts and acts as if the blindfolded eye were never to be used.

Until you are about sixteen years old, your brain continues to develop new pathways and networks from nerve cells. There is a real competition to make connections. Cells that are not sufficiently stimulated—like the case of the eye with the patch—become stunted. On the other hand, cells that are frequently and strongly stimulated may connect with more than one thousand neighbors. They make sure that especially important messages reach the correct address in the brain as fast as possible and trigger the appropriate movements, thoughts, feelings, and memories. This is why you automatically stop as soon as the traffic light turns red, even though you yourself are lost in thought and have forgotten everything around you.

Erwin Neher was born on March 20, 1944. He received the Nobel Prize for medicine in 1991, along with Bert Sakmann, for the discovery of how nerve cells communicate with one another. He conducts research at the Max Planck Institute for Biophysical Chemistry and teaches at the University of Göttingen in Germany.

Why Are There Boys and Girls?

by Christiane Nüsslein-Volhard

Do you have brothers or sisters? If so, you know that every one of you is a little different, even though you have the same parents. If you don't have siblings, just look at your friends—they are all a bit different too. Some have blue eyes, some have green, along with freckles or a dimple, and blond, red, or brown hair. I bet there are a couple of show-offs, maybe a couple of pretty cool kids, but some teacher's pets, too, as well as know-it-alls, worrywarts, superjocks, book-worms, and some who are horse crazy. Then there's the biggest difference of all: Some are boys, others girls.

Why isn't everybody just the same? There would

be so much less stress! People often ask that question, especially when boys and girls, or men and women, start quarreling. But it absolutely has to be that way, for three important reasons. First, boys and girls are there to become men and women. Only men and women, jointly, can have children. The second reason why there are men and women is to guarantee that no two people are exactly alike, not even siblings. (There is only one, special exception to this rule: identical twins.) You'll learn the third and most interesting reason later, because I want to save the best for last.

If you're thinking on your feet, you're now already asking yourself: But why are men and women needed to have children? We biologists asked ourselves the same question, since we know many organisms that need no one else—that can reproduce all by themselves. Bacteria or yeast cells are a case in point. Have you ever watched how quickly yeast dough rises? A clump of baking yeast is mixed with some flour, milk, and sugar and kept warm. After only eleven minutes each single yeast cell has divided into two; after twenty-two minutes there are already four; and if by mistake you left the dough standing for three hours, each cell would have grown into more than eighty-four thousand. And they keep growing as long as the supply of flour and sugar lasts. The yeast cells feed and grow and divide, and in the process, they release carbonic acid gas into the dough and inflate it. So you'd better get the dough into the oven before it grows larger than you!

Plants, too, don't necessarily need other plants to have offspring. From many plants you can take what we call "cuttings"—for example, the broken-off twig of a pussy willow—and place them into a glass of water. After a few weeks roots will have grown from the little twig—a willow baby, ready to go. If you plant it in soil, the twig will grow into a tree. A similar thing happens with some animals. Are you familiar with the transparent jellyfish that float in the ocean and are sometimes washed up onto the shore?

Their mother, who looks totally different, is stuck on the bottom of the ocean. The little jellyfish simply grow from her head and let go as soon as they're ready. Some worms split little pieces off of themselves, from which new worms grow. An earthworm cannot do this, though many people claim it can. If it is cut into two pieces, it must die. The most it can regrow is the very tip of one or the other of its ends that has been lost. Some lizard and fish mamas can have babies without a papa in the picture. So can aphids. So you see: Reproduction among some organisms can occur without male and female joining. They're saved a lot of trouble that way. It's not easy to find a partner.

Many animals have to travel long distances to meet a suitable partner. When one is found at last, there are tests to see if it's the right one. Often it's the wrong one. And even when a little he-mouse finally discovers his little she-mouse, there is no guarantee he'll get her. There are other he-mice, after all, who might be stronger or look better or who were simply there first. But plants can't go meet other plants, which is why reproduction is even more complicated in their case. They attract bees and butterflies with their colorful flowers. A little bit of pollen gets stuck on the insects. When they visit the next plant, bees and butterflies give off some of this pollen and pick up some new pollen, and so on. Flowers that have been fertilized by flying creatures in this roundabout way will grow fruit. The fruit bears seeds, which, once released and sprouting, can finally grow the new little plants. It's all pretty involved, isn't it?

So it's more convenient for many organisms to produce offspring all by themselves. But there's a catch. In nature all creatures who have the same mother and no father are as like one another as eggs in a basket. It's a little boring, of course, when all children are exactly the same as their brothers and sisters—but it could also quickly get dangerous. For if everyone's the same, that means they have the same weaknesses: to winds and bad weather, to enemies and diseases. Assume that all fatherless aphid children liked only the juice from rosebush leaves and nothing else. All would be well as long as enough roses grow in the garden where they live. But once the gardener decides to grow tomatoes in place of those aphid-ridden rosebushes, the aphid sisterhood would starve—all of them, together. Only if a few of them could also stomach the juice of tomato, raspberry, or nettle leaves would at least some of the aphid family children survive. That's why it's so important that all children not be the same—and not only aphid children, but children of all living organisms, including humans. Think of city dwellers trying to protect themselves against robbers. If all buildings used the same lock, a thief could make a copy of a single key and use it to enter any house in the entire city. The residents are protected better if they install a different lock on each house and change locks from time to time.

Have you had chicken pox, measles, mumps, or German measles already? Some children get these contagious illnesses more easily than their brothers and sisters, and some tend to run high fevers. Others don't. This is because everybody has a slightly different "immune system," which is what we scientists call the body's automatic defense system that fights all illnesses. You could compare it to the police force in a big city. If your immune system alone does not succeed in getting rid of a cough or a fever, you can take cough syrup or pills that help you get healthy more quickly. Unfortunately, researchers have not yet found medications to successfully fight some very dangerous illnesses, like cancer or AIDS. Even in the case of these serious illnesses, some people do not suffer from them as much as others do. To this day, nobody really understands why this is so. Most likely, these people simply have a different immune system or something else in their bodies makes them different. So it's obvious: The more we differ from one another, the more likely some of us will find a way out of dangerous situations, no matter what the danger.

One example is enough: When your grandparents were schoolchildren, many childhood diseases, like diphtheria and scarlet fever, were life threatening. At that time vaccinations and medications for fighting the activators of these diseases did not yet exist. Many children who were infected with scarlet fever died, but some won the fight against the contagious agents and survived.

Who actually sees to it, though, that each person is just a little different from all others? The answer: his or her parents. They pass part of their traits on to their children, through their genes. Genes determine what we look like, how we experience things, how we'll grow up, and how we'll die in the end. Each gene carries out a specific task: Some see to it that your bones are strong; others determine whether your eyes will be blue or brown; still others make sure that you can easily digest different things, like meat or jelly beans. Each child receives each gene twice: once from the mother (through the egg cell) and once from the father (through the sperm cell). Both—the mother and the father, too—also have a matched set of genes, because for every gene from their mothers, they received another one from their fathers. Chance determines which of the two in a set of genes is passed on to the child. For this reason, no two children are born with the same combination of traits (except for identical twins).

You don't believe me? Well, then, pretend that the genes are M&M's and that your mother has one hundred of them, fifty yellow and fifty red. Imagine now that you're allowed to pick exactly fifty M&M's—but you have to close your eyes. Which M&M's are you going to pick? All fifty yellow? All fifty red? Thirty yellows and twenty reds? One red and forty-nine yellows? Okay, you've got the idea: How many red M&M's and how many yellow M&M's you'll pick is not yours to decide. It's a matter of chance. You can repeat this game many times in a row; and each time you'll pick a different combination of red and yellow M&M's. A similar thing happened when your mother passed her genes on to you—only you received not fifty but roughly thirty thousand! Now include your father's genes in this picture, and you can see how no two children in the entire world can inherit exactly the same mixture of traits from their parents.

Whether a baby will be a boy or a girl is also decided by genes—or, to be more precise, by a bundle of genes passed along as one package called the "Y chromosome." Only boys have the Y chromosome; girls don't. Because only boys and men have it, only they can pass it on later to their children. Only half of all sperm cells contain the Y chromosome, however. The other half does not. Which of the sperm cells will actually fertilize the mother's egg cell—one with the Y chromosome or one without—is once again left to chance, as when you picked yellow and red M&M's with your eyes closed. That's why fathers and mothers can't determine whether they will have a boy or a girl or what other characteristics their children will have. But one thing is sure: The fact that men and women exist makes for variety among people. Besides, sometimes it's really fascinating to have two sexes and not just one.

It starts in the schoolyard, during recess. "Girls are useless. They just giggle. What a bore," boys might say. "Boys are stupid. You can't really talk to them. All they care about is cars and football," the girls say. Not all boys are rowdy or car fanatics, however. Not all girls are silly either. They can be pretty funny or smart or gorgeous enough to die for—just the right combination for falling in love. Of course, you already know that feeling when you find that a girl is just so cool (or a boy, whichever). You want to know her or him better, spend time together, but you don't dare to really show it. And when you decide to say something, not a word leaves your mouth. That can all be pretty exciting! It's even more so if one or the other finally gets up some courage. Believe me, it's just the same for adults. Without this feeling, without love, life would be half as wonderful—and that's the third reason why we have boys and girls.

Christiane Nüsslein-Volhard was born on October 20, 1942. She was awarded the Nobel Prize for medicine in 1995, along with Eric Wieschaus and Edward B. Lewis, for the discovery of the role of several genes in *Drosophila melanogaster*, the fruit fly. She conducts research at the Max Planck Institute for Developmental Biology in Tübingen, Germany.

Why Does 1 + 1 = 2?

by Enrico Bombieri

One day the owner of a little store in my neighborhood had an idea that was fun. He placed a jar filled with jelly beans on his counter and promised to give the whole jar to anyone who correctly guessed how many were inside. Since I'm a mathematician, of course I didn't simply want to make a guess; I wanted to establish the exact number of jelly beans. But how? With my bare eyes, I tried to estimate the possible size of a jelly bean, the size of the empty space in between the beans, and how large the jar might be. I then started to calculate. Too bad the number I came up with after all my calculations was as much off the correct number as the estimates of most other customers!

We humans can immediately see whether a bowl of fruit has four or five apples in it, but we cannot simultaneously perceive more than ten objects. It's all the more impossible for us to recognize at a glance how many jelly beans fill up a whole jar. Our eyes are just as unable to measure the millimeters between jelly beans. For that, you need special measuring devices. So my attempt to assess the number of jelly beans did not have much chance of success. Still, it's a good example of the way mathematicians approach a problem. We always want to simplify a problem by reducing it to basic units and the relationships between these units—in the case of the jelly beans, to the relationships between the size of the beans, the distance between them, and the size of the jar. You need to know these measurements to be able to make exact calculations of the number of jelly beans.

All of mathematics deals with such relationships. It starts with counting. Although we take numbers for granted, they are based on important rules.

What, after all, do we mean by "counting"? Why does 1 + 1 = 2? you asked me. To understand why, you have to pay close attention to what you do when you count. How do you count the jelly beans in the jar? You remove one and put it on the table. Then you take a second one and place it next to the first. If someone now asks you how many jelly beans you removed, of course you answer, "Two"! When counting, we combine both jelly beans in our mind and say: "Here are two jelly beans." We write it down as 1 + 1 = 2.

This first step of going from one thing to the next is the foundation of counting. After that first step it simply continues. Take another jelly bean from the jar, and 2 + 1 jelly beans are on the table. That, we call "three jelly beans" and write as 2 + 1 = 3. Therefore, counting means moving along from one number to the one that immediately follows. This principle of using numbers can also be stated like this: Start with the unit of 1, add another 1, you get 2, add another 1, you get 3, and so on. We mathematicians say that 2 follows 1, or 3 follows 2, and so on. As such, $1 + 1 = 2$ is a statement meaning nothing other than 2 follows 1. Besides the principle of succession, counting has additional basic rules. It does not matter whether you first take two jelly beans and then add three or whether you take three and then add two. The order does not matter. Either way, you wind up with five jelly beans. The mathematical equation looks like this: $2 + 3 = 3 + 2$.

Once you understand the basic rules of counting, you can derive other rules. For example, $2 + 3 = 5$ becomes what we call a "mathematical proposition." In other words, you can prove $2 + 3 = 5$ simply by applying the basic rules. I will save this proof for the end, however. Of course, you'll ask: But why do we have to prove something as simple as $2 + 3 = 5$? I think in a way you have a good point in this case. For no one is seriously going to claim that $2 + 3 = 6$. Our experience as mathematicians has proven, however, that all propositions need to have a proof—easy ones as well as difficult ones. More than one large system of theories has collapsed like a house of cards because apparently obvious relationships later proved suddenly wrong. The field of mathematics is quite exact. Every step, no matter how small, has to be substantiated; otherwise, everything threatens to get out of control. To avoid that danger, mathematicians have developed—over the course of the more than three-thousand-year-old history of their science—their very own, precise language. Thanks to this language, every mathematician has the possibility of checking what other mathematicians have come up with. This kind of critical review, though, can be very difficult at times: Some mathematical proofs are so complicated that they take up hundreds of pages.

The disadvantage of such a highly specialized language as mathematics is that regular people, unfortunately, rarely understand anything of what is being talked about. Even experts, when they are listening to their colleagues, sometimes feel transported into a country whose language they do not speak. The field of mathematics has grown so much that nobody can know all of it. Luckily, there are areas of inquiry in mathematics that can be described in simple terms. For example: Is there a largest number, with no larger number following? The answer is no, because you can always add 1, and there is your larger number. The sequence of numbers—1, 2, 3, and so forth—is therefore "infinite," as we say. The fact that sequences of numbers are infinite leads to a strange phenomenon: You cannot write down most of the really, really large numbers, even if you thought up extremely smart abbreviations. We would simply run out of materials to write them down—there would not be enough paper and ink in the whole universe to write down all of these monster numbers! Our understanding of such very large numbers is extremely limited. We know they must exist, but we can't really imagine them.

Interesting problems in mathematics are found not only in very large numbers. What's small is also exciting. Quickly, take a ruler that measures centimeters. You'll see that every centimeter is divided into ten equal parts, called "millimeters." This kind of division is based on the decimal system. It is also used when we write down numbers: We write all of our numbers with ten digits: 0, 1, 2, 3, 4, 5, 6, 7, 8, and 9—for instance, the year 2003 or the decimal fraction of 0.33333 . . . (This is the fraction that results from dividing the number 1 by 3.) Now you can once more divide each millimeter into ten equal parts—at least, in your mind—and then again, each of these new parts into ten equal parts, and it can go on like that forever. You've got the idea: Applying this simple "divide-in-ten-parts" rule leads us quickly to difficult questions, just as in the case of very large numbers.

Over the centuries mathematicians learned to enlarge the realm of what could be regarded as a number. They discovered a really important principle in mathematics: It makes no difference whether we represent something—say, a length—in algebraic terms as 0.5 or in geometric terms as 1:2. Just as a photo of your friend is not really your friend but only a representation of him, the mathematical description of something is not the thing itself. You are able to recognize an object or a person, however, based on a description, if it fits the most important aspects. If I tell you, "Why don't you ask the man with the red tie holding a yellow book in the crowd over there?" you know whom I mean. If I say only, "Why don't you ask the man in the pants?" there would be many different men fitting that description.

Over time, people realized that it was not the single objects that mattered in mathematics, but rather the way they related to one another, the so-called mathematical relationships. The objects as such are unimportant. In my view, all of mathematics is nothing but the study of these relationships. The mathematician investigates above all the nature of these relationships, or, as we say, their "structure." He wants to discover which of the relationships are really basic and suitable as building blocks for other relations—just as, in the beginning of this chapter, we pursued the structure of the numbers 1, 2, 3, and so on, as they related to one another.

After this excursion into abstract mathematics, I'd like to give you an example that illustrates how different objects can have the same mathematical relation. The rings of the planet Saturn, which you may have seen in a photograph or on TV, consist of many chunks of rubble and ice that are circling around Saturn. Hundreds of years ago, the French mathematician Laplace considered the rings more closely and wondered why, in fact, they do not fall apart. Laplace investigated. He calculated the stability of Saturn's rings and developed an equation that describes a state of equilibrium, now named the "Laplace equation." Later on, it became clear that this Laplace equation plays an important role not only in astronomy, but also in building a telephone network that is able to make all of its users happy. And what do telephones have to do with Saturn's rings? Nothing! But the mathematical relationships that describe a well-functioning telephone network and those describing the equilibrium of Saturn's rings are the same. Both obey the Laplace equation.

For the last forty years, I have also been working to solve a riddle. It has to do with so-called prime numbers—that is, numbers that are divisible only by 1 or by themselves. Examples of prime numbers are 2, 3, 5, 7, and 11. You can quickly check it yourself. Any even number, of course, except for 2, cannot be a prime number because it can be divided by 2. Therefore, except in the case of 2, prime numbers must be uneven, and you can prove that there is an infinite number of them. But what's so interesting about prime numbers? you might ask. Well, they are the building blocks for all numbers. Every number is the product of prime numbers—the ancient Greeks knew that already. It means that any multiplication of numbers can be brought back to a multiplication of prime numbers. Here is an example: 25 x 33 = 5 x 5 x 3 x 11.

As you'll remember, the rule for the sequence of numbers starting with 1, 2, 3 was very simple: Begin with 1 and keep adding 1. If you tried to use a similar rule with prime numbers, it wouldn't work: Start with 2, then comes 3, 5, 7, 11, 13, 17, 19, 23, and so on. If you take a prime number and look for the next one in line, there is no clear rule for how to find it. Certainly, you could make a list of prime numbers by going through each number and checking each to see if it can be divided by more than 1 or by itself. That is not a rule, however. And it would not be all that easy. Remember the monster numbers I talked about earlier? Checking even a "small" one with, say, forty digits could take up your whole life. Only sophisticated computer programs will solve this kind of task sometime in the near future. That's why huge prime numbers could be used as secret numbers on the Internet, for example, if you wanted to transfer money. Prime numbers do an excellent job disguising messages, because they are so hard to analyze. The fact that large prime numbers could play an important role in day-to-day business was a surprise for me as well.

Even more fascinating than a list of prime numbers is the question: Do prime numbers appear at random within the sequence of all numbers or according to some hidden rule? The best mathematicians have searched for such a rule. Bernhard Riemann, a German, discovered 150 years ago what this rule might look like, and although to this day nobody has succeeded in proving his conjectures, most mathematicians believe they are correct. But why is it so difficult to prove Riemann's assumption? That is a mystery that I, too, am trying to solve. Meanwhile, there are more and more indications that something fundamentally new might be concealed in it. For this reason, the problem of prime numbers is considered the most important unresolved puzzle in mathematics. A puzzle like this—the kind that everyone is breaking their teeth on—of course provides a great motivation for many young people to learn the language of mathematics. Once you have grasped this language, extraordinary thought possibilities open up. Of course, everything in mathematics has to be correct, but it provides tremendous freedom. Just as art does. Once a painter has learned the techniques of painting, he himself can decide what his brush will or will not paint on his canvas.

What is technique in mathematics? you may wonder. I'll now demonstrate it by outlining the proof I promised you. The proposition was that $2 + 3 = 5$. In order to substantiate this proposition, all we have to do is prove that $2 + 3 = 4 + 1$, because $4 + 1$ follows 4 and is therefore 5. We make our proof in three steps. We know that 2 follows 1—that is, $1 + 1$; and 3 follows 2—that is, $2 + 1$. Therefore, we can write it in another way: $2 + 3 = (1 + 1) + (2 + 1)$. The parentheses refer to the fact that the numbers in them are to be added first. In the second step we replace the remaining 2 with $1 + 1$ (because 2 follows 1), and we wind up with $(1 + 1) + ((1 + 1) + 1)$. In order to take it a step further, we now need another basic rule of counting: The way we place the parentheses does not matter. In other words, we can write $(1 + 1) + ((1 + 1) + 1)$

or we can write (1 + 1 + 1 + 1) + 1. We now have finished our proof, because 1 + 1 + 1 + 1 = 4; therefore, 2 + 3 = 4 + 1, or the number that follows 4.

Many people do not care for something that is as exact as this little proof. Others are immediately taken by this kind of logical thinking. If you are one of them, look for good books that are fun and that inspire you to want to know more—more than why 1 + 1 = 2. The field of mathematics is as varied as a garden of countless flowers and plants.

But don't ever forget: As great as this science may be, it is not all. There are more important things in life—above all, one's humanity. I myself am the father of a handicapped child. Although she is deaf and mentally retarded, she is a wonderful human being. I have learned more about life from her than from a combination of all the mathematical theories I have studied since childhood. My daughter is the best thing that could have happened to me in my life.

Enrico Bombieri

Enrico Bombieri was born on November 26, 1940. He received the Fields Medal in 1974 for his groundbreaking contributions to various mathematical problems. He lives in Princeton, New Jersey, where he teaches at the Institute for Advanced Study. The Fields Medal is awarded only once every four years and is considered the highest honor in mathematics—the equivalent to the Nobel Prize, which, unfortunately, is not given in mathematics.

How Much Longer Will the Earth Keep Turning?

by Sheldon Glashow

So you want me to tell you how much longer the Earth will keep turning? That's a really good question, because people have been wondering about it for as long as we have been able to think. I myself became a physicist only because in high school I never understood exactly what the Earth and the moon were doing. So I decided to find out myself. You'll have to pay close attention from this point on since not everything I'm going to tell you is all that easy to understand. Even the smartest people have racked their brains trying to find answers to your question, without succeeding.

What we do know is that the Earth turns around

its own axis. What I mean by "axis" is an imaginary line leading from the North Pole to the South Pole, right through the center of our planet. Everything turns with the Earth—people, too. We don't feel it, actually, because the Earth is so huge and this movement is terribly slow, too slow for us to perceive it. One way you can know that the Earth actually is turning is because there is morning and evening. As the Earth turns and the place you live with your parents is exposed to the sun, it becomes day, and when it turns away from the sun, night sets in. Just picture a spinning top. It, too, will turn if you give it enough of a twist. Unlike spinning tops, though, the Earth does not only turn in place, but it moves at the same time in a circle around the sun. If you look closely, you'll find that the circle is not actually perfectly round, but rather an ellipse. An ellipse is a line that looks as if it had been drawn around an egg.

It's easiest for now if we imagine three globes: one of them the Earth, one the moon, and one the sun. Each one is not only turning about itself, but it is also always moving along its so-called orbit. The Earth orbits the sun. Once around takes one year. The moon orbits the Earth. Once around takes about four weeks. And the sun orbits the center of the Milky Way, the incredibly huge space that contains the sun, the moon, and all the stars in our galaxy. It takes the sun roughly 250 million years to get around once in the Milky Way. That is such a long time, we can't even imagine it.

If you're interested in how much longer the Earth will keep turning, you're bound to want to know as well how it all got started. Unfortunately, none of us knows exactly. We assume that many billions of years ago it started with a huge explosion, the "big bang." Atoms were formed as a result, then matter, and from it came into existence the solid stuff that in turn formed the planets that circle the sun. We can only have a vague idea of when the sun came into being because we're dealing with time frames beyond the grasp of our imagination.

The planets I mentioned are not the planets we

know today. We only know that they existed because our Earth and all the stars we see in the night sky originated from them. This is what happened: The very first planets broke apart the way cookies break, because enormous forces pushed upon them. As a result, dust, debris, and rubble whizzed through space. These materials formed clumps that then created new formations: satellites, planets, and meteors. Today, all three are familiar to us: Our moon, for example, is a satellite, the Earth on which we live is a planet, and a meteor is a huge chunk of matter that streaks through space, which you sometimes see as a shooting star.

We don't know why the Earth rotates around its own axis. It simply does, although there's no need for it to do so to keep within its orbit. At this point I should mention again that there are many things in space we cannot, unfortunately, explain. We know that things are the way they are but not really why. Most likely, we'll never find out about many of these things. I believe that people like to talk about God for this reason, about an almighty creator who made the universe, the planets, human beings, animals, and plants on the Earth. The thought of a higher power that understands everything we don't comprehend is a kind of comfort to us. Even so, there have always been extremely bright people who have studied our world and discovered things about it. One of them was Isaac Newton. He lived in England a long time ago and discovered that a rigid, firm body that moved in a straight line would never stop unless a resisting force got in its way. An important precondition is that the body is rigid and firm. We call this "Newton's law of motion," and I'm sure you'll learn about it in high school in physics classes.

You see, it's not an easy task at all to answer your question. We have to talk about lots of other things first. But we are slowly approaching our goal. We know now that movement can be stopped by resistance. Resistance could be the ground or water, or it could also be air, even if that seems strange to you. Just stick your hand out of a moving car—what do you feel? Resistance! Precisely. Every ball, every stone, every brick soon stops moving once it falls to the ground, for example. In space these things would continue to fly about. Space—where the sun, moon, and Earth are moving around—has no air, so there's no resistance. Why does the moon orbit the Earth and the Earth the sun? That's easy to answer! They attract each other, just like magnets. You can conceive of each planet basically as a magnet. In theory, the sun, Earth, and moon move toward one another and would eventually touch one another if they were not so incredibly far apart. The force with which they attract one another is not strong enough. The moon is about 240,000 miles from the Earth, and the sun about 93,000,000 miles. None of us can fathom how huge these distances are. I'm sure, though, that on TV you've seen a reporter in Europe ask a question of a fellow reporter in the United States. They're so far apart from each other that there's a delay until the question arrives. It takes only fractions of a second, but we notice it. That is because the question has to travel by means of radio connections to satellites that hover above the Earth and then all the way back again to Earth. If we were to ask a question of an astronaut on the moon, it would take about one second until the question arrived. It would take eight minutes to reach the sun. That's how far away it is.

All right, we now know that the Earth, moon, and sun continue to move because there is no resistance in space, and that's where they chase about. This is where it begins to become interesting. I'll explain to you shortly why, despite all this, the Earth will not go on turning until the end of time. You remember that Newton said that movement continues forever if we're dealing with a rigid and firm body. The Earth, however, is not rigid. Think of it as a chocolate with cream filling and several layers: a fluid center, an in-between layer, a coat, a crust, and a sheath—that's the layer of air, or atmosphere, above us. Above that is only space, which has no air. You know that some things in the atmospheric layer move, because you see clouds drift and winds blow. You also have to know that there's movement within all layers of the chocolate. Part of this movement goes in the opposite direction from the Earth's surface. And because, in a way, all the layers are floating, one on top of the other, moving and doing extremely weird things, the Earth is not a rigid body.

Now think only of one layer, the crust. That's what we move on and what we can see: the land and the oceans. The crust is the thinnest of all the layers of the chocolate. Seventy percent of it is covered with water. The largest expanses of water are the oceans. They have high and low tides. Before I go on and tell you more, I'd like you to conduct an experiment: Take a big plastic bowl, fill it with water, and jostle it a little. If you now try to slide the bowl sideways, you'll realize that it takes you more energy than if the water in the container was still.

Alas, our Earth is slowly losing energy because it has to move around with all that tidal water constantly sloshing about. Because of this, it keeps turning more and more slowly. It isn't much slower—maybe just a fraction of a second each year. Nonetheless, years become longer as a result. Because of this, we are always having to adjust our clocks. When dinosaurs were still alive, the Earth moved at a faster pace. A day was only about twenty-three hours long at that time. At some point, a day on the Earth will be twenty-five hours, then twenty-six hours, and so on. And because of this, there will be a point in time when the Earth stops moving. Don't start worrying, though, because a seemingly infinite amount of time has to pass before this will happen.

In the meantime, something will happen with the moon that will also play a role: It will move farther and farther away from the Earth. Its force of attraction will weaken because it, too, will rotate more and more slowly around its own axis. We can measure this distance by sending signals to the moon and waiting until they come back. It takes longer today than in the past—only by the tiniest of tiniest fractions of a second, but still, it takes longer.

So the Earth turns more and more slowly and the moon moves farther and farther away. What will happen in the future is only a guess. We physicists believe that the moon, after getting off its current orbit, will move back toward the Earth. Are you kidding—why should it turn around and come back? you may now ask. Good point, but it will happen all the same, because the moon will have moved closer and closer to the sun, and the sun will send it back. You simply have to believe me. I had to study all of this for many years before I could comprehend it myself. To really explain at this point all that is involved would get too complicated.

Eventually, the moon will come so dangerously close to the Earth that enormous forces will act upon it and break it to pieces. All its parts will rain down on the Earth and destroy it. You needn't fear for your families or friends, though, because uncountable millions of years will have to pass before this happens. I believe that by that time, the human race will have long found a new universe with a new sun, a new

Earth, and a new moon. And they will have the opportunity to travel there. I have no idea where that will be. But we have enough time, after all, to find out.

Sheldon Glashow was born on December 5, 1932. In 1979 he received the Nobel Prize for physics, along with Steven Weinberg and Abdus Salam, for their description of electromagnetic interactions. He teaches at Harvard University in Cambridge, Massachusetts.

Acknowledgments

Have you ever spoken to a Nobel Prize winner? No? Well, it's not too easy to get involved in a conversation with a Nobel laureate. I came to know some of these elusive people during my research for a series of articles in the *Süddeutsche Zeitung Magazine*, which later evolved into the work for this book. I was on the phone with them, we exchanged letters and e-mails, and because a lot of Nobel laureates live in the United States, I frequently had to get up in Munich at 2:00 A.M. to have conversations about the benefits of cell division, the insanity of war, or the blue of the sky.

Once, I even participated in a real conference of Nobel laureates. It took place in the beautiful city of Lindau on Lake Constance in Germany, during the summer. The sun was so hot that all the Nobel laureates had taken off their jackets and, with them, their conference name tags, which were now draped over so many chairs! At the time I arrived, they were all sitting on the terrace of the old Bad Schachen Hotel. They were eating strawberry pie and talking about the benefits of cell division, the insanity of war, or the blue of the sky. But how do you recognize a Nobel laureate without a name tag? The faces of Michael Jordan or Madonna are well known, but you don't usually recognize the faces of Erwin Neher, Paul Crutzen, Richard Roberts, or most of the other laureates—unless they are Mikhail Gorbachev or the Dalai Lama.

First, I approached an older gentleman with a high forehead and gray hair. He was rather delighted to meet me, but he was a retired manager for a corrugated cardboard plant in Amsterdam who was spending his first vacation after retirement at Lake Constance. That was my first and last mistake. I don't know exactly how I recognized them, the very smartest people of our era. Perhaps it was something about their eyes. The way

Nobel laureates look at the world seems focused and directed outward while at the same time focused deeply inward: an expression that is curious yet restrained, almost introverted.

In the end, many of them agreed to take part in the project. They were willing to try it. They were to find answers once more to all the difficult questions they had already solved, this time in ways understandable to all of us, children included. For this, I am deeply grateful to all of them and I want to thank them, not least because I realize the special challenge this undertaking presented. For once they were required to direct their attention to the outside world only.

Perhaps, dear reader, you will be surprised, but nearly all Nobel Prize winners are modest and shun the public limelight. They are not particularly keen on public appearances. Fortunately, those represented in this collection took the risk anyway and proved to us that people like them are at least as important as Michael Jordan or Madonna.

My gratitude also goes to all those who took part in making this book a reality. I thank Christian Kaemmerling, who had the idea, and my friend and colleague Gabi Herpell's son Johnny, whose questions for the Nobel laureates were always the best.

I would also like to thank the following people for their hard work, which has made it possible for this book to be published in English and so reach a much wider audience: Susan Danziger, my agent in New York; Ginee Seo, my editor and publisher at Atheneum; Ann Bobco and Russell Gordon, who made the book beautiful; and Jeannie Ng, whose diligence kept us from making too many mistakes. And finally, my thanks to the translators, Paul De Angelis and Elisabeth Kaestner, whose meticulous work on this book made every contributor's voice a delight to read.

—Bettina Stiekel, Hamburg, Germany, April 2003

Made in the USA
Las Vegas, NV
17 March 2021